# Old-Time Farm and
# Garden Devices

## and How to Make Them

## Rolfe Cobleigh

*Illustrated*

DOVER PUBLICATIONS, INC.
Mineola, New York

*Bibliographical Note*

This Dover edition, first published in 2005, is an unabridged republication of all the text and drawings from the work originally published in 1909 by Orange Judd Company, New York, under the title *Handy Farm Devices and How to Make Them*. The black-and-white photographs have been omitted from this reprint for space considerations.

*International Standard Book Number*

*ISBN-13: 978-0-486-44400-0*
*ISBN-10: 0-486-44400-7*

Manufactured in the United States by LSC Communications
44400708   2019
www.doverpublications.com

# By Way of Introduction

SUCCESS comes to the man who so works that his efforts will bring the most and the best results—not to the man who simply works hard. It is the know-how, things-to-do-with and economy that count. Labor-saving machinery has revolutionized many a trade and industry. It has made farming an industry and a science of possibilities undreamed of and unattainable a hundred years ago. But it is not enough for the modern farm to be equipped with the best tools and machinery that shops and factories turn out, to know how to use them and keep them in repair. There are many handy devices, not made in any factory and not sold in any store, that every intelligent man can make himself, which save money and labor and time. Inventive men are constantly contriving simple but valuable things to meet the needs of their own practical experience. We are all the time hunting after and gathering these ideas. Now we are putting a lot of the best ones into this book. We are trying, by words and pictures, to explain clearly just how to make each device. Everything described is tried and practical. Some are old, many are new, all are good for the purpose intended. They represent the practical, successful experience of farmers and other wide-awake workers all over the United States.

This book is broader than its title. The over-flow of good measure includes a valuable chapter on the steel square and its uses. Nowhere else has this subject been handled in a way so easily under-stood, with confusing mathematics cut out. We especially commend this chapter to our readers. We also present some good house and barn plans, that will be appreciated by those who contemplate building.

In addition to the direct benefit to be derived from doing what the book tells how to do, we have in mind the larger purpose of education toward putting more thought into our work and doing what we have to do the easiest, the cheapest and the quickest way. Out of it all, we trust our readers will make progress toward greater pros-perity, greater happiness and greater usefulness.

# CONTENTS BY CHAPTERS

# · WORK · SHOP · ·AND·TOOLS·

## THE FARMER'S WORKSHOP

THERE is no doubt that of all the handy farm devices good tools head the list. So, in this book, we are going to start with carpenter tools and the place to keep and use them. Every farmer ought to have a workshop in which he can do odd jobs and make things when the weather prevents out-of-door work, or at times when there is little to do on the form. Economy and thrift demand that a farmer should have and keep in good condition a few essential carpenter tools. First of all he should have a long, strong, smooth-top bench and, either on racks above the bench or in a tool chest, he should keep in order, and where he can easily find them when wanted, his stock of carpenter tools. Some of the tools that will be found useful are the following:

A rip saw, a crosscut saw, a back saw, and a compass saw; a jack plane, a fore plane, and a smoothing plane; a shave or drawing knife; two or three chisels of different sizes for woodworking and a cold chisel for metal; a gouge or two; a good hatchet; two or three hammers, including a tack hammer and a bell-faced claw hammer; a brace or bit stock with a set of half a dozen or more bits of different sizes; one or more gimlets; a mallet; a nail set, a large screw driver and a small one; a gauge; a spirit level; a miter box; a good carpenter's square—No. 100 is a good standard size;

7

compasses or dividers; cut nippers, a pair of small pincers and a pair of large ones; a rasp; a large, flat file; at least one medium-sized three-cornered file and a half-round file.

It is poor economy to buy cheap tools. Of course extravagance is to be avoided, but be sure that you get first-class material in every tool you buy. It is a good plan to get a good practical carpenter to assist you in selecting your tools. Keep on hand in the shop a variety of nails, brads and tacks, screws, rivets, bolts, washers and nuts, and such small articles of builders' hardware that are likely to be needed occasionally, including hinges, hasps and staples and some sand-paper. Have a good plumb line, chalk and pencils. Keep in a handy place a jar of a good liquid glue, and some cement. See to it that the shop contains a good stock of well-seasoned lumber, both hard wood and soft.

Attached to the bench should be a bench screw or vise. This need not be an expensive one, but should be of good size and strong. There should also be a pair of carpenter's saw benches, a shaving horse, a small anvil and a grindstone. Every farmer has a grindstone somewhere about the buildings, but it is a great convenience to have a good one in the workshop.

A corner of the shop should be devoted to painting supplies, including several colors of good standard ready-mixed paints and stains, raw linseed oil, boiled linseed oil, turpentine, varnish, putty, points for setting glass, several brushes of different sizes, a good putty knife and panes of glass of different sizes ready for emergency.

A farmer ought to be able to do occasional little jobs of soldering. He needs soldering iron, a bar of solder, resin, a little bottle of soldering fluid, which can be purchased already prepared, also a small sheet-iron furnace in which to heat the soldering iron.

It would cost quite a tidy sum to buy all these things at once, but they can be gradually accumulated as one is able to purchase them, and then the outfit should be kept complete. Whenever anything in the shop is broken, worn out, or disappears it should be replaced.

Whenever farm implements or anything about the barn or house are broken or out of order, they should be properly fixed. Often a few minutes spent at the right time will make a thing almost as good as new, while, if neglected, it may soon get beyond repair and have to be thrown away. A thrifty farmer always keeps his farm implements well housed and in repair. It is not what we earn, but what we save, that makes us rich. It is quite as important to stop the leaks as it is to figure on big profits directly.

## RUNNING THE GRINDSTONE

If the face of the grindstone is hard and glazed pour a little sand on the stone every few minutes until the glaze is worn off and the stone will cut like a new one. This condition is caused by exposing the stone to the weather. It is best to keep the stone in a shed under cover, but if this is not possible, set it under a tree and put a box over it when not in use. It is surprising how easy a little oil on the bearings will make the stone run. A few drops of kerosene will cut the gum if it runs hard and then some oil or axle grease will make it go easy.

It is hard to stand on one foot and work the

treadle with the other. The job can be made easy
by bolting two boards to the grindstone frame, and
extending it 2 feet, on which place a seat as shown

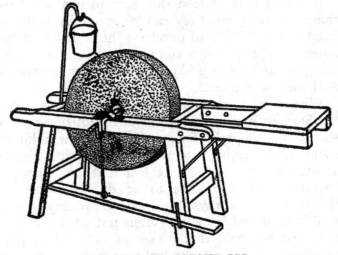

HANDY GRINDSTONE RIG

in the cut.    An uneven stone needs to be cut down
and toned up. This can be done by grinding against
the end of a piece of pipe, having the stone dry.

---

Good nature is as contagious as the measles. Put
on your best smile when you get up in the morning
and observe how everybody will greet you with a
sunny face.

---

## A HOMEMADE ANVIL

A homemade anvil can be constructed from a
4-foot piece of railroad rail mounted on a trestle, as
shown in the sketch. This affair will stand a lot

of heavy pounding, and comes in handy in many ways. The rail is just about the right shape to make an anvil.

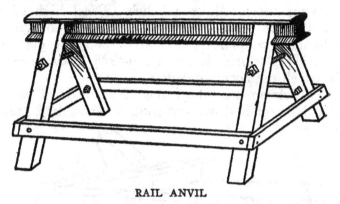

RAIL ANVIL

## MAKING A NEW TOOL

A very handy wrench for many kinds of work, such as making gates and contrivances, where small bolts are used, is shown in the cut. From a small monkey wrench remove the wooden handle, and weld the metal part to an old bit-stock, as shown in the cut. This permits of very rapid work in screwing up small bolts. Where there are so many things to do as there are on a farm, it pays to do things in the easiest and quickest BIT-STOCK WRENCH way. This is one of the real time-savers.

---

Learn to live, and live to learn,
Ignorance like a fire doth burn,
Little tasks make large return.—Bayard Taylor.

## HOW TO MAKE A SHAVING HORSE

One of the most useful devices on a farm is a shaving horse. Make a bench 18 feet high of a good 2-inch plank, *c*, level off the edges so that it will make a comfortable seat. Upon this place a slanting platform, *b*, through which is cut a hole in which the clamp, *a*, works.

The clamp must be made of heavy hard wood that is tough and will not split. The shank, *f*, must

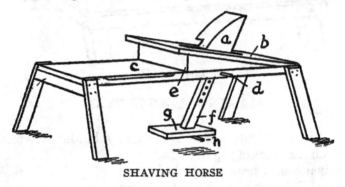

SHAVING HORSE

be an extension of the clamp, *a*. Several holes in the plank will allow the clamp to be raised so as to take in larger pieces of wood. The treadle, *g*, is kept in place by a peg at *h*. To operate this horse the workman places his foot upon the treadle, inserts the wood to be clamped under the edge of *a*, and pushes backward upon the treadle. This clamps the wood and the drawing knife can be used readily and much more rapidly than with a vise.

## A CONVENIENT FARM HORSE

On the farm there is continual use for such a horse as is shown in the drawing. Not only when doing little jobs of carpentering, but also in many other operations, such a support is found necessary. This little horse is an improvement over the ordinary stiff affair, in that it shuts together when not in use, and so can be packed out of the way.

HORSE READY FOR USE

It is made of boards cut in strips, the two horizontal boards at the top being hinged together, as shown herewith. While in use the legs are kept apart by long hooks, as may be plainly seen in the picture.

---

When tillage begins, other arts follow. The farmers, therefore, are the founders of human civilization.—Daniel Webster.

---

## A WIRE SPLICER

The neatest and strongest splice can be made with this little instrument. It is a strip of iron 1 inch wide and ⅛ inch thick. One end is cut narrow and is bent into a hook large enough to fit neatly the largest wire to be spliced. At the sides of this two notches are filed, as shown at the left. At the right the splicer is seen in position on the wire. The splicer should be turned backward, as it appears in the right-hand drawing, to make the splice. A pair of large pincers o r a v i s e s h o u l d be used to hold the two wires between the coils while turning the splicer. The

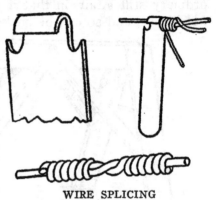

WIRE SPLICING

splice as finished appears above. The length of the handle may vary. If the splicer is to be used for net wire, of course the handle cannot be longer than the width of the mesh. Otherwise, 6 or 7 inches is about right for No. 8 wire. If it is to be used only for small wire, the length of the handle should be reduced for the sake of convenience.

## SERVICEABLE HOMEMADE LEVEL

A serviceable level is shown in the illustration. Take two 1-inch boards of rather hard wood, well-seasoned, 2 to 3 feet long, bolt or screw them together at right angles. This union must be so strong as never to be moved by ordinary pressure. At the top of the perpendicular piece cut a slit and insert a piece of strong thread. To the bottom of the thread tie a thin circular

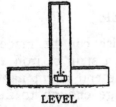

LEVEL

weight. Lay the device across two trestles of nearly the same level. Just above the weight mark the place where the string hangs. Reverse the position of the instrument by turning it end for end, and again mark the position of the string. Half way between the two marks place a third. When the string hangs over this mark the lower board will be level. A shield of tin may be placed over the weight. A nail on each side of the string, just above the weight, will keep it from swinging far out of place. It must be allowed to swing freely.

A simple level may be improvised by filling a small flat bottle with water, so that only a bubble of air remains, and attaching it lengthwise and near the middle of a straight stick or narrow board.

## TO MAKE A HANDLE STAY ON

To secure the handle of a hammer or ax is often quite a bothersome problem. A special wedge made

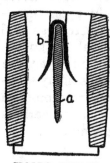

HOLDS WEDGE

with a piece of wood as at *a*, in the sketch, held in place by a fence staple, *b*, has been devised to meet the need for a wedge that really holds. The prongs of the staple should be bent slightly outward before it is driven in, so that they will spread in the handle. There is little danger of handles coming loose when they are attached in this manner, and it is little more difficult to set a handle as indicated than in the old-fashioned way.

## A TOOL BOX REQUISITE

Among the handiest things to have in the tool box are some small bolts about 2 inches long with thumb nuts. A dozen or so of these will prove their value many times over in the course of a year. In making tables for fairs or suppers or in any sort of knock-down arrangement, or temporary convenience where strength is essential, nothing surpasses a bolt of this description. With a brace and a bit the right size, one may be entirely independent of nails and screws.

A farmer friend of ours was once called upon to make a fence about a child's crib without any marring nails. A slot in the fence post with a thumb bolt just above the crib line gave an alligator jaw result which was very satisfactory. On another occasion a knock-down stage was carried from the storeroom in pieces and put together by two men in 20 minutes. An actual computation of its strength showed that a locomotive might safely run over it.

The man referred to above has 100 feet of tables for hall purposes, depending entirely upon the 2-inch bolt and thumb nut for their fastenings and braces. There is never any trouble about knocking out nails. To one having a brace and bit these handy things will suggest of themselves many satisfactory uses. A supply of iron washers should be kept in hand, and in time a collection of various sizes of wooden washers will accumulate.

## SOLDERING

Soldering may be done by anyone having a very simple outfit. All that is required is a copper soldering iron, some solder, a vial of muriatic acid and some resin. A fairly successful job of soldering a tin dish may be done by scraping the surface bright where the hole is, sprinkling on a little finely powdered resin, laying on a bit of solder and holding the dish over a flame, which may be from an alcohol lamp, until the solder melts. It will cover the hole and stick. If the dish is rusty or badly tarnished use muriatic acid in place of resin. Resin works best when tin is bright, but usually solder sticks most successfully when the acid is used.

For soldering large breaks or doing important jobs of soldering the iron must be used. In order to work well the iron has to be kept coated with solder. When it gets blackened it should be filed until bright and then rubbed upon a smooth board -while hot in a mixture of melted solder and resin. When the hot iron is taken from the fire wipe it on a damp cloth before trying to use it to lift the melted solder. A soldering iron is best heated in charcoal or the coals of a wood fire. The copper should never get red hot, as that causes the coating of the point to be burned off. The metal to be soldered must always be heated before the solder will unite it.

Solder may be obtained in bars at any tin shop. It can be made by melting together 2 parts of lead and 1 of bar tin. This is the usual proportion for most purposes. Soft solder that will melt quickly and can be easily used for mending tinware can be made of pure lead and tin in equal parts. A hard solder is made by melting together 2 parts of copper to 1 of tin. Brazing solder is made by melting together brass and one-sixth its weight of zinc. When cool it should be granulated by pounding with a hammer.  For soldering steel and iron to brass the following combination of metal is melted together, 3 parts tin, 39½ copper, and 7½ zinc. Before it is applied, all the metals to be jointed together must be heated to the same temperature as the soldering alloy.  Gold solder is made of 24 parts gold, 2 parts silver and 1 part copper.  A hard silver solder is made of 4 parts silver to 1 of copper.  A soft silver solder is made of 2 parts silver to 1 of brass.

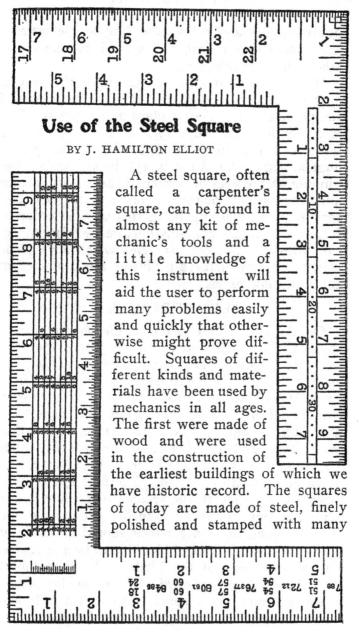

# Use of the Steel Square

BY J. HAMILTON ELLIOT

A steel square, often called a carpenter's square, can be found in almost any kit of mechanic's tools and a little knowledge of this instrument will aid the user to perform many problems easily and quickly that otherwise might prove difficult. Squares of different kinds and materials have been used by mechanics in all ages. The first were made of wood and were used in the construction of the earliest buildings of which we have historic record. The squares of today are made of steel, finely polished and stamped with many

figures, tables and rules, according to the taste of
the manufacturer and the special mechanic for
whom they are designed.

We will not attempt to deal with the several
special kinds or makes, taking up only a few of
the possibilities of the standard 2-foot square. This
is 2 feet long on the blade, which is two inches
wide, and it is 16 or 18 inches on the tongue or
angular leg. The latter is 1½ inches wide. Beginning at the heel or corner of the square, inches
and fractions of inches are marked. It is necessary that the marking be in this way, in order to
form the different combinations desired in connection with the different problems which have to be
solved. A few of these problems are explained in
the following pages.

## LUMBER RULE

On the side of the blade of the square that is
divided into inches and eighths is placed the lumber rule or scale. This is used for computing the
number of feet in board measure contained in a
given board or piece of lumber. We show a
picture of a section cut from the center of
the lumber rule. The space running lengthwise of the blade between the parallel lines
contains the number of feet board measure
for a given width of board. The first space is for
boards 8 inches wide, the second for those 9 inches
wide, the third for those 10 inches wide and so on.
To determine the space which should be used for
any given width, look under the 12-inch mark on
the outside edge of the blade. These numbers
give the width of the board, also the number of feet
board measure. If a board is 10 inches wide and
12 feet long, it contains 10 feet board measure.

Now let it be required to find the number of feet board measure in a board 13 inches wide and 11 feet long. Find the space for boards 13 inches wide under the 12-inch mark on the square, follow this space to the left and under the 11-inch mark on the square will be found the answer desired: 11—11. This is read 11 feet and $\frac{11}{12}$, and is the number of feet board measure contained in a board

| 1 1 | 1 2 | 1 3 | 1 4 |
|------|------|-------|-------|
| 7-4 | 8- | 8-8 | 9-4 |
| 8-5 | 9- | 9-9 | 10-6 |
| 9-2 | 10- | 10-10 | 11-8 |
| 10-1 | 11- | 11-11 | 12-10 |
| 11-11 | 13- | 14-1 | 15-2 |
| 12-10 | 14- | 15-2 | 16-4 |
| 13-9 | 15- | 16-3 | 17-6 |

LUMBER RULE

13 inches wide and 11 feet long. With a little practice, anyone can measure lumber or timber and check up his bills for this kind of material.

Do not confound foot board measure with square feet. Square feet are in surface measure, with no reference to thickness, while a foot board measure is the equivalent of a foot square and 1 inch in thickness. The square feet of a 3-inch plank would contain 3 feet board measure.

After becoming familiar with the use of the lumber rule, as described above, you will discover that the space may be taken to contain the amounts for a given width and the different lengths in feet as represented in the different columns, or the space may be taken as containing the amounts for a given length and the different widths arranged in columns; therefore, find either length in feet or width in inches under the 12-inch mark and follow this space until under the inch mark representing the other measurement. In this space will be found the feet board measure.

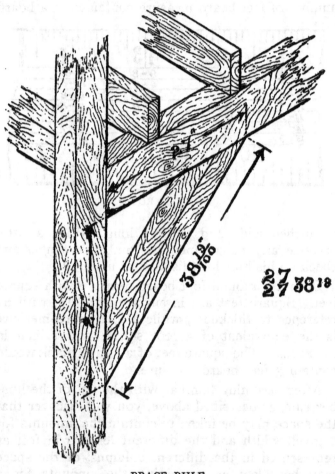

BRACE RULE

## THE BRACE RULE

The brace rule is on the tongue of the square, and has a series of figures representing the rise or vertical height, the run or horizontal reach and the true length of a brace. For example, they are written $^{27}\!/_{27}\,38^{19}$ and $^{45}\!/_{45}\,63^{64}$. These would be read 27 inches run, 27 inches rise and a length of 38 and $^{19}\!/_{100}$ inches, and 45 inches run, 45 inches rise and a length of 63 and $^{64}\!/_{100}$ inches.

A glance at the illustration on page 22 will give a good idea of the application of the brace rule as it appears on almost any modern make of square.

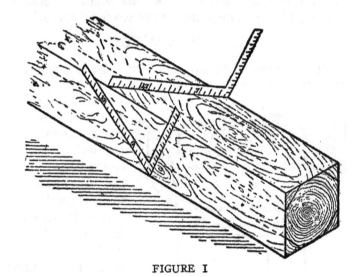

FIGURE I

## THE OCTAGON SCALE

There is an octagon scale on one side of the tongue of the square, but we will not attempt to explain its use, as there are easier and simpler methods of obtaining the same result.

One method is shown in Figure 1. To obtain the lines on a square stick where the corners should come when converted into an octagon or eight-sided stick: Lay the square on the one side of the square stick at such an angle that the end of the square will come exactly at the edges or corners of the stick, make a dot on the 7-inch mark and at the 17-inch mark. Through these dots gauge or mark a line parallel with the edge of the stick. Continue this operation on all of the four sides. This gives the lines for the corners of an octagon. In making a flag-pole or spar for a boat or to round any large stick this is the operation used by all mechanics doing the work by hand.

## THE MITER BOX

Of all homemade devices, one of the most frequently used in the shop is the miter box. After

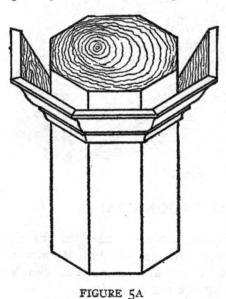

FIGURE 5A

the box is put together it is a simple problem, with the use of a steel square, to make the cuts necessary to intersect two pieces of wood, as shown in Figure 2. First, the box must be straight and true and the sides form a perfect right angle or square with the bottom. Lay the steel square on the top of the box so that the 12-inch mark on the blade and the 12-inch mark on the tongue will both come

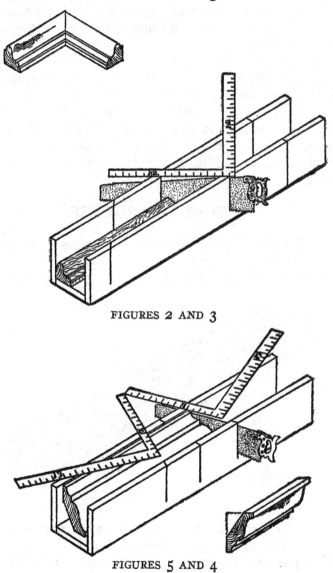

FIGURES 2 AND 3

FIGURES 5 AND 4

exactly on the edge of the box. This gives the miter cut of the intersection of the angle of a perfect square, as shown in Figure 2. Figure 3 shows the manner of placing the square on the box to give the desired angle.

A sprung molding, which is a molding not solid on the back, as shown in Figure 4, must be placed in the box bottom side up as shown in Figure 5, so as to get a solid bearing to hold it. Cuts in the box to miter around an eight-sided figure or an octagon, as shown in 5A, can be obtained by using 7 inches and 17 inches, marking the cut on the 7-inch side, as shown in Figure 5.

## TRUING THE SQUARE

After obtaining a steel square, the first and most essential thing is to test or prove it to see that it is accurate, forming the angle of a perfect square.

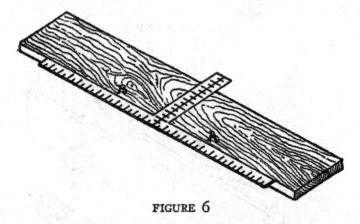

FIGURE 6

Take a board planed on one side and straighten one edge of it perfectly as described under Making a Straight Edge. Make a mark across this board with the square, as shown in Figure 6, Position A, then reverse the square to Position B. If the square is true it should exactly fit the mark made. It is necessary to work very accurately, making the mark with the point of a knife and having the edge of the board absolutely straight.

If the square is found to be out or inaccurate, it is not necessary to throw it away; it can be made true by a simple method by any handy mechanic. If you do not possess an anvil, make a substitute by

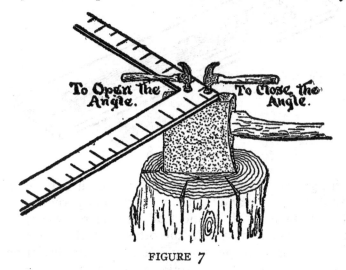

To Open the Angle.    To Close the Angle.

FIGURE 7

sticking the ax into a chopping block, lay the square on the head of the ax so that the bearing will come from the throat or inside angle to the heel or outside of the square. To close up the angle, strike with a hammer a sharp blow at a point near the heel; to open the angle, strike near the throat at a point indicated in Figure 7. Don't strike too hard. Use a bell-face nail hammer and the dent will not be noticed.

## A STRAIGHT EDGE

In connection with the work with the steel square a straight-edged board is necessary to have ready for immediate use. Procure a board 8 or 10 feet long of good, dry pine, free from knots and 6 to 8 inches wide. Plane the edge until it seems

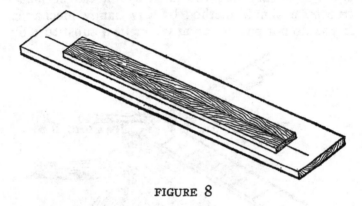

FIGURE 8

straight to the eye, then lay it on the bench or on another board and make a mark along the edge, just straight with a fine lead pencil; reverse it or turn it over and fit it to the other side of the pencil line. This multiplies any inaccuracy or deviation from a straight line. Make a new line each time you plane the edge. Work with as long a plane as you have and set the blade to take a fine shaving. When the edge will fit both sides of the line made from it while in one position, it is straight. Figure 8 will give a clear idea of this operation.

## RAFTERS

The common rafter for a pitch roof is easily laid out with the steel square. There are many methods, but the easiest and most simple is by spacing. Two dimensions, half the width of the building and the height of the roof, are divided into an equal number of parts. The width of half the building is called the run and is usually divided into parts of 12 inches or a foot for convenience. The height is called the rise, and is divided into an equal number of parts. A glance at Figure 9 tells us that the run there shown is 10 inches rise to 12 inches run.

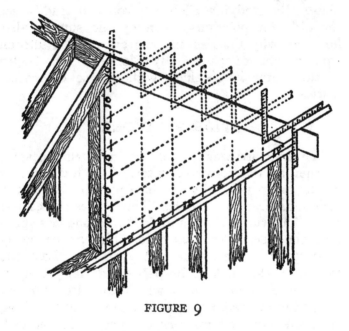

FIGURE 9

When the square is laid on the stick to be cut into a rafter, the 10-inch mark on the tongue and the 12-inch mark on the blade are held so that they come exactly even with the outside edge. The blade then takes a level position and the tongue a vertical position or plumb position. This gives the proper level for the cut at the top of the rafter and the level cut at the top of the plate. As the square now lies on the stick make a fine mark and move the square along, marking another space. Mark as many of these spaces as the parts into which the rise and run were divided. This gives the length of a rafter from the ridge to a point exactly over the outside of the plate.

Where the rafter overhangs the plate, it is necessary to square down or in to form the notch for the plate. By studying Figure 9 you can readily see the different positions taken by the square, also, how and why the rise and run are divided into an equal number of spaces. By this method the length of the rafter is obtained without use of mathematics.

## STAIR STRINGER

The stair stringer is laid out in much the same manner as the common rafter. The total rise of height to go up is divided into parts of about 7½ inches, as near as possible. This makes the easiest step. The run is always divided into one less space than the rise. The reason for this can be easily understood by examining Figure 10. Lay the square on the stick to be used as a stair stringer, taking the numbers into which the rise and run have been divided, mark, and slide the square along until the required number of spaces are marked. A little experience, with allowance made for the surrounding conditions, and any handy mechanic can lay out stringers for an ordinary flight of stairs. To get an easy flight of stairs for the person of average size where plenty of room can be used, experience teaches that 7½ inches rise and 10 inches run or tread makes an easy flight.

From this some stair-building experts have put together the following rule, which works very well for the average stair: When the rise multiplied by the tread equals 75, the run will be an easy one, as 7½ inches rise by 10½ inches tread equals 75; 8⅓ inches rise by 9 inches tread equals

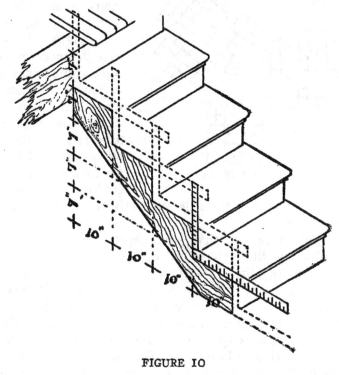

FIGURE 10

75; 8 inches rise by 9½ inches tread equals 76, which is very near the desired result. When the rise is 9 inches or over, the rule is not good, as the tread must be shortened up much more, and the rise should never be more than 11 inches—that is about the rise in an ordinary ladder leaning against a house.

## THE 47TH PROBLEM OF EUCLID

The problem shown in Figure 11 is known as the 47th Problem of Euclid, and is an invention by an

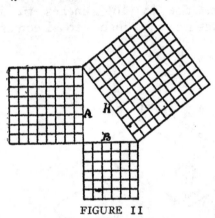

ancient Greek geometer who sought many years for a method of finding the length of the hypothenuse of a right angle triangle in mathematics, and when the method was discovered, history tells us there was great rejoicing. Pythagoras is credited with having

FIGURE 11

first proved the rule successfully applied to the problem.

The rule is that the square of the base added to the square of the altitude equals the square of the hypothenuse. The base of a right angle triangle is the side on which it rests, marked B in Figure 11. The altitude is the height and is marked A in Figure 11. The hypothenuse is the connecting side of the triangle, marked H in Figure 11. The base, 6, squared or multiplied by itself, equals 36. The altitude, 8, squared, equals 64. By adding these together we have 100, which is the square of the hypothenuse. It remains but to extract the square root of 100, which we know is 10, therefore 10 is the length of the hypothenuse or third side of this right angle triangle. All right angle triangles can be figured in the same manner, but only multiples of the length of the three sides come even—such as 3, 4, 5 and 12, 16, 20, as shown in Figure 12; and many others, of course.

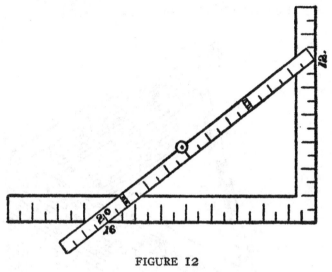

FIGURE 12

## THE RULE OF 6, 8 AND 10

This is a rule so extensively used in the building trades and others that it has finally come to be known by the above name. It is derived from the 47th Problem of Euclid, and is used in the manner shown in Figure 13.

Measure 6 feet on the end sill of a building and 8 feet on the side sill. If it measures 10 feet across the angle the building is square. This is a very useful rule and easily remembered. It is always available in running lines for batter boards for masonry or lines for walks. By starting from a corner stake into which a nail is driven, measure off on the string or line used and insert a stake to mark the place. Drive a nail into this stake and

proceed in like manner on the other side. With a
little care and practice, quite a job of surveying
can be done by using a few stakes, a ball of string
and a tape or 10-foot pole.

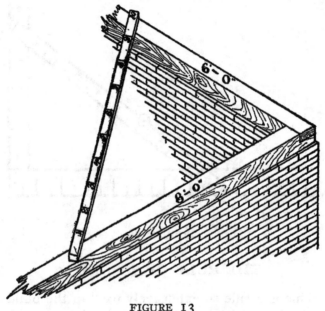

FIGURE 13

## ANGLES

An angle is the opening between two lines meet-
ing at a point. Angles are usually spoken of as being
of a number of degrees. The degrees are measured
on the circumference, the center of which is on the
point of the angle. There are 360 degrees of the
circumference of a circle. The surface of the earth
is so divided north and south by the parallels of
latitude, which are numbered from the equator each
way; also east and west by the meridians of longi-

tude, which are numbered from Greenwich, England. They can be seen on any map.

By the use of a protractor, the number of degrees of any angle can be obtained. Figure 14 shows one-half of a circle or 180 degrees.

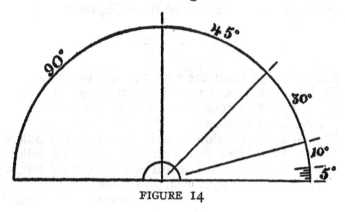

FIGURE 14

## PLOTTING ANGLES

To strike an angle in a field on a large scale where one line is given or can be obtained, measure off from the point of the angle 57⁸⁄₁₀ feet; lay one

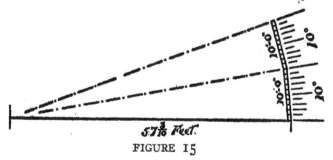

FIGURE 15

end of a 10-foot pole at this point. The other end should be swung around so that it also will be 57⁸⁄₁₀ feet from the starting point. Each foot marks off 1 degree on the circumference of a circle whose radius is 57$\frac{3}{10}$ feet. If more than 10 degrees are required, continue as before, keeping the ends of the 10-foot pole always on the circumference of the circle from the starting point. A clear idea of this operation can be obtained from Figure 15.

---

Labor is rest from the sorrows that greet us;
Rest from all petty vexations that meet us,
Rest from sin-promptings that ever entreat us,
   Rest from world-sirens that hire us to ill.
Work—and pure slumbers shall wait on thy pillow;
Work—thou shalt ride over Care's coming billow;
Lie not down wearied 'neath Woe's weeping willow!
   Work with a stout heart and resolute will!
                 —Frances S. Osgood.

# IN and AROUND the HOUSE

## THE STEP-SAVING DUMB WAITER

ONE may save many steps in every house where the kitchen is situated over the cellar, to say nothing of other considerations, with a small outlay of time, and perhaps, without the expenditure of a single dollar, by means of a dumb waiter, which may be placed in any convenient corner out of the way. A handy size for an ordinary family is 2 feet square with four shelves, counting the top, 1 foot apart. These shelves may be hung from the corners, the center or the middle of the sides, by means of manila sash cord over pulleys placed close to the ceiling of the kitchen and nearly balanced with weights, which should be confined in a little case. They should be guided in ascending and descending by means of grooves in the middle of the sides extending from top to bottom of the inclosed case. In the cellar the case may have a fine

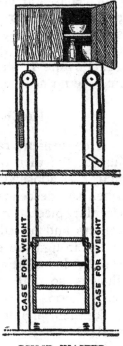

DUMB WAITER

wire screen door and in the kitchen an ordinary
cupboard door or one with a glass front, as desired.

The doors should slide upward and be balanced
like an ordinary window with sash weights and
pulleys. In order to prevent the waiter from descending when being overloaded a pivoted wooden
latch, as shown on the right-hand side, should
engage with the ends of the shelves, and to prevent any shock from too quick descent some coiled
springs should be placed at the bottom of the case.
If desired a small cupboard may be built at the top
of the case for storing little-used articles.

Some advantages of such a waiter are that food
may be placed on the shelves and lowered into the
cool cellar and either allowed to stay there or removed to the refrigerator. Thus it will be unnecessary to carry anything to or from the cellar, and
this will often mean a saving of several trips up
and down. If the cellar is clean and cool there
may be no need to use a refrigerator or an ice box.

## RACK FOR PRESERVES

A convenient rack for preserves may be made
just at the turn of the cellar stairs in a house, so
that the housewife need not step off the stairs,
when she descends for a can of preserves. Several
circular pieces of wood are pierced through the
centers and nailed to a kind of wooden shaft that
runs through the entire rack. Nail barrel hoops of
the thick, wide variety around the edge of the
shelves, so that the contents cannot fall off. The
barrel hoops are soaked in water for several hours to
make them pliable, so they can be fitted around the
shelves.

In a socket at the bottom, the middle shaft slips,

the upper end working in a socket in the end of a stout piece of wood nailed to the beam overhead. The sockets may be purchased at the hardware store. The glass cans are arranged on the shelves, and the housewife can stand in one spot and turn the rack around until she finds the jar for which she is looking.

From the covers of large cheese boxes anyone could make a similar rack, using it in attic or kitchen, anywhere where one wants a rack which will hold an extra large number of articles for the amount of space involved.

---

Ill husbandry braggeth
To go with the best:
Good husbandry baggeth
Up gold in his chest.—Tusser.

---

## TRANSFORMING A WASHSTAND

The kitchen cabinet here shown was made from an antiquated washstand and table, using old lumber, odds and ends of varnish, nails and screws, the finished article costing less than 50 cents. The only tools used were a saw, hammer, plane and square, such as can be found in any farmer's collection.

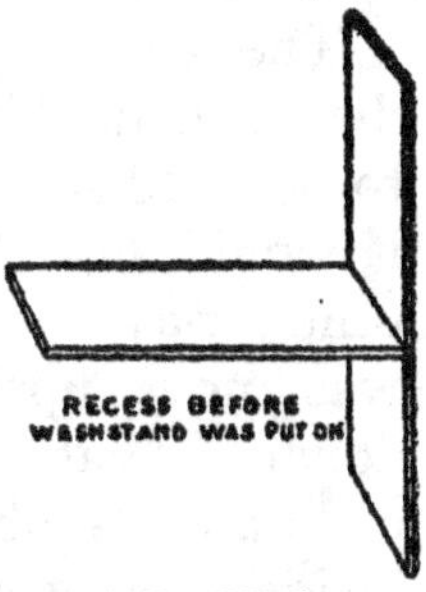

First, the shelf shown in Figure I was made, it being wide enough to reach each end of the table and deep enough for the washstand to set on it flush. To the right end

RECESS BEFORE WASHSTAND WAS PUT ON

FIGURE I

was screwed a board of the same width, the shelf being so placed that it would be 2 feet above the

WASHSTAND AS IT WAS

table. A board of equal width formed the support at the other end.

Then the washstand, from which the top had been removed, was placed upside down on the shelf (*bbb*), one end of the washstand reaching to the extreme left end of the shelf, and the two were securely fastened together. This left a narrow open space between the right end of the washstand and the right support of the shelf. A board was then nailed on top from one end to the other, and a back added.

The drawer of the washstand had to be fixed so that it would slide the other way, as it was now upside down. That necessitated a shelf inside the washstand above the drawer. Old lumber was used, and

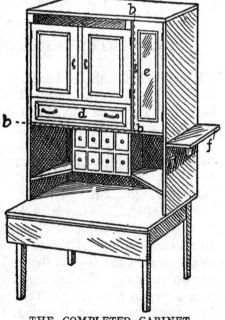

THE COMPLETED CABINET

this was smoothed with a plane, then sandpapered and holes and cracks filled with putty. When the putty was dry it was sandpapered again.

A support was then nailed to the back of the recess for a spice cabinet. This left the cabinet about 4 inches from the table. This support also did for two shelves, one in each corner of the recess. The spice cabinet contained eight small drawers and added much to the whole. A door with a glass sash (e) was then made for the narrow space to the right of the washstand above the recess. This made a little china closet with two shelves and containing over a dozen brass cup hooks. The space near the top on the left-hand side, between the short legs of the washstand, was left open for the crumb and draining trays. A piece of batten was nailed around the top as a finishing touch.

A leaf, which could be raised when required, added to the table room. The cabinet being placed in a corner left the front and one end free. On this end or side were placed two salt boxes, one for salt, and the other for kitchen cloths. Directly above these and reaching the length of the end was a shelf (f) for the clock, etc. Finally, walnut varnish stain, two coats, was applied. In each side of the recess were screwed two large cup hooks. Similar hooks were screwed on the inside of the washstand doors, to hang up biscuit cutter, corkscrew, nutmeg grater, etc.

## HOMEMADE DRESSER

Sometimes it is necessary to use homemade makeshifts in the house furnishing, and sometimes it is done through a desire to exercise one's ingenuity in fashioning simple affairs. The accompanying illustration shows a plan for making a simple dresser that when finished will not only be very useful in itself, but will also add a useful bit of furnishing to the room.

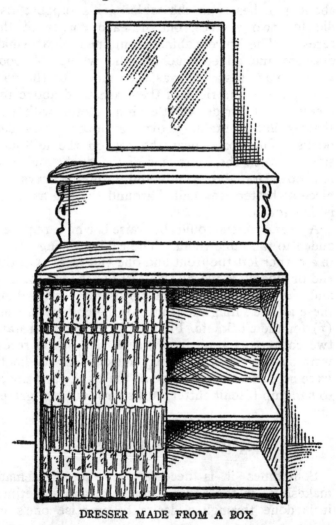

DRESSER MADE FROM A BOX

Select a drygoods box of the right size to fit well into the space to be utilized, then fit two shelves to the interior, as suggested. The whole box should be covered on the outside with some pretty cloth, the edges being drawn over and around the front edges of the box, and neatly tacked inside. Make a shelf with a length equal to the width of the box and fasten it to the wall above the box with some pretty nickel brackets, as shown in illustration. Cover the shelf with cloth, also. Now place a looking-glass above the shelf and have a curtain like the covering in front of the opening. This curtain can have little brass rings sewed to the upper edge, which will slide on a small brass rod.

Dost thou love life? Then do not squander time, for that is the stuff life is made of.—Benjamin Franklin.

Earth is here so kind, that just tickle her with a hoe and she laughs with a harvest.—Douglas Jerrold.

Blest is the man whose wish and care
Is just to be happy anywhere.

## KITCHEN WINDOW CABINET

Nothing lightens labor so much as cheerfulness, and cheerfulness may often be secured by very simple means. In the accompanying picture is shown one way that works well. Instead of the usual kitchen table a cabinet is built below and at the sides of the kitchen window and the top made large enough to serve as a table. In this way the wife may have a pleasant view when she looks up from her kitchen work.  It is not necessary to go into details concerning the construction of such a cabinet, because no two people would be satisfied

CABINET AT WINDOW

with the same plan.  The plan shown is merely suggestive for the thoughtful wife and the handy man to work out to suit their own particular needs.

## TO LET IN MORE LIGHT

Many farm kitchens and dining rooms are dark and gloomy.  It is not an easy matter to cut new windows in the outside wall, though this can often be done to great advantage; but where there is an outside door in a dark room, conditions can very easily be improved, and that, too, at small expense. Doors vary greatly in the manner of construction, some having wide panels at the top and some having two narrow ones of varying lengths. But almost every panel door that was ever constructed can be treated in the way which we will describe. The two upper panels can be removed, and their place filled with two lights of glass. If the door is of modern make it will be found that the wooden panel is held in place by a narrow molding all about it, both inside and out. Remove the molding on one side, and take out the panel. Put in the glass and replace the molding, and the work is done. If, however, the door is of older manufacture the molding on either side may be found to be a part of the door frame. In this case, cut the molding away on one side, neatly and evenly, and remove the panel. Then insert the glass, and having made, or bought, a little strip of molding, fasten it neatly in place around the glass with brads.

In the case of some doors the two panels could be removed, and also the upright between them, leaving a large rectangular opening, into which a single sash of four, or nine, lights could be inserted, the joints being made tight about it with putty and white lead. Then tack a narrow bit of molding about the sash, both inside and out, and a door that will give light to the room will be the result. An outside door looks better with glass in the upper half, and the interior will certainly be made more cheerful and healthful because of it.

---

We know what we are, but know not what we may be.—Hamlet.

## A BARREL CRADLE

Anyone who can use a hammer and nails and needle and thread can make this inexpensive, accessible, easily moved, and cool yet sheltering cradle.

Secure a nice white sugar barrel, clean it thoroughly and remove half of both heads. Place the barrel on its side, removing half the staves, and leaving the other half to form the bed of the cradle.

BARREL READY TO TRIM

Next remove the hoop that is second from the bottom, and then two hoops will be left at the top to form the frame for the hood, and one hoop at the bottom to form the foot. (See illustration.) Carefully nail the remaining staves to the hoops, clinching each nail securely.

Now cover the frame thus formed, as shown in the accompanying illustration. Any thin cotton goods that may be laundered can be used. Figured lawn would be very pretty, and if economy is an item, a worn bleaching sheet will do. Place a little mattress or pad and a tiny pillow within, or the usual cradle furnishings may be used. One yard of mosquito netting stretched over the opening of the cradle will prevent insects from bothering, and the netting itself cannot touch and awaken the baby.

FINISHED CRADLE

## TO PROTECT BABY FROM HOT STOVE

Winter months mean extra care for the mother of a baby, but possibly the greatest of the additional cares that winter brings in this regard is that of keeping the curious tot from the hot stove. Build a pen around the stove to protect him from it. The pen is a simple affair. It consists of four little gates, made just large enough to surround the stove, and covered with netting. The wire netting does not interfere with the free passage of heat and is very effective in keeping baby from getting burned. The gates are made of 1¼-inch strips, mortised or neatly fitted. For netting use ordinary poultry wire of 2-foot width. The gates are held in place by hooks and screw eyes. This arrangement is better than hinges, as it makes the taking down of the affair, for sweeping or cleaning the stove, much easier.

In the summer you may use the gate at the foot of the stairs, across the porch door, and in other places where baby is determined to go, and where he is in danger of falling and getting hurt unless protected in this way. For this pen, the lumber costs 25 cents, the netting 25 cents, and the hook and screw eyes 15 cents, making a total of only 65 cents.

## A BOX FOR CLOTHES

In many of the furniture stores one may see pretty cloth-covered boxes that are used in bedrooms as a receptacle for various articles of apparel, the inside, as well as the outside, being covered with pretty figured cloth. The inside of the cover is fitted with pockets for slippers and slumber shoes. These little chests are so light that they may be lifted about with one hand.

To make such a chest, select one of the very light and well-made grocery boxes in which cereals and various brands of breakfast foods are shipped, which may be had at any grocery store. See that the corners and the bottom are nailed securely. The top will be composed of at least two pieces of board, and these can be made into a solid cover by nailing two cleats beneath them. But these will not look very attractive when the covering is being put on, so a more workmanlike plan will be to saw off a couple of inches from each end of the top boards and supply the place of the wood removed by nailing along the ends a 2-inch strip of the same thickness. This gives a cleat at each end, but the cleats in this way form part of the cover itself.

Use long wire nails to secure these end pieces in place.

It will be a simple matter to cover and line the box when the covering material is at hand. Use very small tacks and carry the outside covering up over the top and down over the inside, which will make the use of tacks along the top unnecessary. The lower edge of the cover can be tacked on the bottom of the box, so the tacks will not be seen on the outside at all.

## SCOOPS FROM TIN CANS

Scoops for handling sugar and flour are among the most convenient utensils that one can have about the pantry; and in a short time a good supply may be made from materials that are going to waste about almost every home.

Take an ordinary tin can and either melt or cut off the top. With a pair of tinner's shears (a strong pair of household shears may be used), begin at the open end and split the side of the can to within about an inch of the bottom. Opposite this one make a similar slit. Parallel to the bottom of the can, cut from the lower end of one slit to that of the other. Round the corners of the remaining half, and the body of your scoop is finished.

For a handle, about 4 inches off the end of an old broomstick is just the thing. If this is not available, a handle may easily be shaped with a knife from a piece of soft wood. To attach the handle, from the inside drive a small nail through the center of the bottom of the can and into the center of the handle.

Some additional strength is obtained by planning so that the seam of the can will run down the middle of the lip of the scoop, thus stiffening it. A salmon or corn can makes a very convenient sized scoop for the sugar, while tomato cans serve very nicely for flour and meals, and half-gallon paint buckets may be thus utilized for handling light materials.

## A HOMEMADE FOLDING TABLE

A handy game or sewing table may be made as follows: Take two planed boards 12 inches wide and 3 feet long. Fasten them together with two

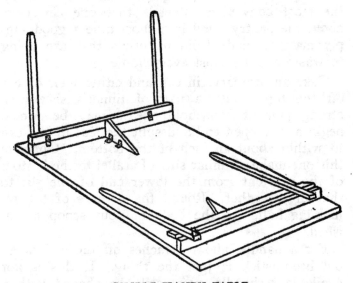

SIMPLE HANDY TABLE

strips 2 inches wide and 24 inches long. Fasten these strips by strong screws in upright position. Now take two similar strips and fasten them by hinges to the pieces screwed on the boards. Fasten four stout legs to these in the manner shown in the cut. Take two three-cornered boards large enough to hold the legs stiff when dropped into position, and fasten them by hinges, as shown.

The same general plan may be followed in making a much larger and heavier table or a lighter one.

## A HOMEMADE BUTTER WORKER

A butter worker is one of the handy devices that should be upon every farm. A good type is shown in the drawing. It is made of close-grained hardwood—maple or birch are recommended—tight-jointed, free from knots and perfectly smooth in size. It slopes enough to drain readily at the narrow end through a short piece of lead pipe inserted

BUTTER WORKER

at the bottom. The working bar has a strong, smooth iron rod or spike at its lower end, which is easily inserted into or removed from the hole in which it works. The part of the bar that comes in contact with the butter is half-round on one side and two flat sides meet at a right angle. Of course, it must be as smooth as possible.

## HOME CHEESEMAKING

Nearly every farm home contains, or may easily be supplied with, the necessary appliances to make cheese, and it is not a difficult task when one is once familiar with the process. For a small batch of about 12 gallons of milk the following method is a good one: Take about 6 gallons of the evening's milk and leave it covered with a cloth in a

CHEESE PRESS

temperature of 65 to 70 degrees until morning and then mix 6 gallons of morning's milk with it in a large tub or boiler. All milk may then be heated together to 80 to 90 degrees. Care must be used not to get it too hot or to expose it to a draft so that it will cool quickly.

Another good method preferred by some is to use 11 gallons of perfectly sweet morning's milk and to this add 1 gallon of milk that has soured and thickened. The sour milk should be stirred well to get out all the lumps and left for about 15 minutes before the rennet is put in. The easiest way to heat the milk is to place it in a wash boiler right on the stove until it gets up to 86 to 90 degrees and then raise it from the stove by placing it on two bricks. The stove must not be too hot.

Rennet in the form of tablets is most convenient and useful for home cheesemaking. Dissolve one tablet in half a glass of cold water and add to the milk after it has been heated and stir well for two minutes. Some cheesemakers use two or three tablets, as it saves time, but for beginners two are usually enough. If you have liquid rennet extract, use about two tablespoonfuls.

## Cutting the Curd

The rennet will curdle the milk and the curd will be ready to cut in 20 to 40 minutes. This can be determined by noting if the curd breaks clean like jelly when raised on a knife blade. The cutting can be done with a wire toaster, a long knife or a heavy wire. Cut lengthwise of the vessel and then crosswise until the curd is in nearly uniform pieces of ½-inch squares. After cutting, leave the curd on for five minutes, then heat slowly to 100 degrees, stirring all the time. Cook for about 40 minutes at as near 90 degrees as possible, stirring occasionally to prevent the curd from sticking together. Keep the heat up and do not allow the mass to cool.

To determine when the curd is ready, take a handful and squeeze it in the hand firmly and if it feels elastic and does not stick together, it has been cooked long enough. If the milk is good, the curd

should have a pleasant, slightly acid odor.   As soon
as the curd is cooked, draw off the whey or dip off
the curd with a sieve and place in another vessel.
After the curd is well drained and before it sticks
together, add ¼ pound of fine salt and mix well.
After salting, let it cool for 15 minutes, stirring
occasionally, when it is ready for the hoop.

## Pressing and Curing

For a cheese hoop, one can use a tin hoop 7
inches in diameter and 12 inches deep or an old
peck measure without a bottom if holes are punched
in the sides for drainage.   For a press a device
shown in the sketch will serve well, the pail at the
end of the lever being filled with stones.   Before
the curd is placed in the hoop, line it with
cheesecloth, one piece the size of the bottom
and another around the side.   Turn the upper
edge of the cloth over the edge of the hoop
and fasten it tight.   When the curd is packed
firmly, put a piece of cloth on the upper end and
fold it over tight.   Make the pressure slight at
first, but after an hour rearrange the cloth and
make the pressure heavier.   The pressing should
be finished by the next day.   Do not press in too
cool a place, but keep the temperature about 50
degrees.

For curing, set the cheese in a damp room or
cellar which has an even temperature.   Turn it
around daily, and if it shows signs of molding, rub
occasionally with butter.   It should be ready to eat
in three or four weeks.   Cheese will cure at 40
degrees, but it takes longer than when warmer.
Twelve gallons of milk should make about 10
pounds of cheese, according to richness of milk.

After one or two attempts any housekeeper should be able to make good cheese by this method. It is necessary to keep all utensils very clean and the liberal use of boiling water with a little soda will accomplish this purpose.

## WASHES WHILE READING

Here is a way of making play of wash day. Perhaps some of our bright boys will try this to help mother. A friend of ours had an old bicycle unfit for use. He made a frame to raise the hind wheel from the floor, wound the rim with twine (tire being off) and reversed the seat. In place of the form he inserted a piece of pipe (a stick would do as well). Then he took some old belting, cut it

PEDAL POWER DEVICE

to 1¾ inches wide and about 10 feet long, and with that he runs the washing machine for his wife. He can read the paper while he washes, and he does not lose much time from field work either. An emery wheel can also be run with it by bolting 1-inch strips to the top part of the frame extending over the wheel and mounting a polishing head on same.

Knowledge is power.—Bacon.

## TREAD POWER IN THE DAIRY

While the small gasoline engines adapted to running cream separators have been hailed with delight by many dairymen, the old tread power is still a very economical and reliable source of power. With a heavy sheep, dog or the dairy herd bull

SEPARATOR RUN BY RAM POWER

enough power can be produced to run the separator and churn at practically no cost except for the tread.

One difficulty has been to secure a uniform rate of speed, but this is solved if a heavy flywheel is attached to the tread. While the sketch shows a direct drive from tread to separator, a more desirable arrangement is to have the tread located in a room adjoining the separator room, where the milk will not be exposed to the breath of the animal.

---

A great many men wear themselves out devising schemes to sidestep honest work.

## A LAMP FOR COOKING

A lamp may be utilized for cooking purposes in the following way: Make a tripod by taking three strips of wood of equal length, putting in one end a headless nail and making slightly slanting holes in the corners of a 6-inch triangular piece of board in which to fit them. A screw hook in the center of the board, on the under side, completes the device, which has only to be stood over a lighted lamp to be ready for work. A small stew kettle, or tin pail, hung on the hook, within a half inch of the lamp chimney, enables one to have a "pot boiling" in short order. If you have a large lamp, with a round wick, it will give the heat of two or three common ones, and you can cook almost as rapidly as over a stove.

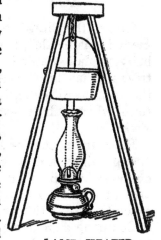

LAMP HEATER

With an ordinary lamp, food can be heated, eggs boiled, or coffee made very quickly, helping wonderfully in the getting of a meal. This is also an easy and convenient way to heat baby's milk, or water, in the night, in case of sickness. Stood on a chair by the table, the device can be used to keep the coffee or chocolate hot during meal time. A round piece of sheet iron, with chains attached to suspend it from the hook, is an additional help, to hold a steeper for tea.

As this tripod can be taken apart readily, when not in use, it will be found a good adjunct to a camping outfit, even though you carry a camp stove, for there will be times when nothing will be wanted but a hot drink, which can be made over the lamp with less trouble than it would be to make a fire in the stove.

## HOT WATER ALL NIGHT

One of the things that must be had quickly when medicine is needed, and still more often for a bottle baby, is hot water at night. The following contrivance has been found to be worth many times the trouble to make it, for it saves annoyance at a time when baby's worrying may mean hours of sitting up.

Place the socket of a wall bracket lamp just high enough above a table so that the top of a hand lamp chimney will be 5 or 6 inches below it. Make an arm of round iron or small piping long enough to extend out over the lamp and to this hang a hook, on which hang a small teakettle or pail. In this enough water for the needs of a night can be kept hot without boiling, and will be ready at an instant's notice. As a night lamp is a necessity in a house where there is a youngster, the cost of this device will be nothing, for the blaze of a small burner will provide sufficient heat. The proper height for the socket on the wall can be determined by measuring the hook and the kettle to be used. The lamp chimney should not be nearer than 2 inches to the bottom of the kettle, or the water will boil and steam away.

## HOW TO CUT BREAD EVEN

Here is one of the most useful devices to which the handy man can give his attention. It is very rarely that a housekeeper can cut even and handsome slices of bread, however much she may desire to have the bread plate look attractive. One slice will be thin, another thick, while another will be thick on one edge and thin on the other. The drawing shows a simple arrangement by which all the slices of bread can be cut of an even thickness without any slant.

Cut a piece of pine board to about 9 x 13 inches. Near one end, on either side, insert firmly two

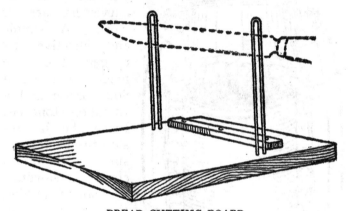

BREAD CUTTING BOARD

pieces of very stout wire, bent double, as suggested in the cut. These wire supports should be at least 7 inches high, and should have another inch of length firmly inserted in the wood. The wire should be as stout as No. 12, or larger still, and should stand exactly at right angles to the board. Put them far enough apart so the largest loaf will readily go between them, and have the opening in each wire standard just wide enough so the knife will slide up and down without " wobbling " The dotted lines show the position of the knife when in place. Screw a little strip of wood in front of the wire, just far enough ahead to make the slice of bread the right thickness. Press the loaf up against this guide and cut off a slice, then press the shortened loaf up again, and repeat the process.

## HOMEMADE WATER COOLER

It's a mighty nice thing to have a good supply of cold water at the barn when threshers, corn

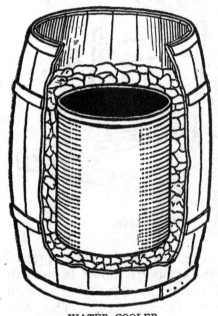

huskers, or hay harvesters are at work. A simple and effective arrangement can be made by using a flour barrel and a 10-gallon stone jar. Place the jar inside the barrel and surround it with charcoal, sawdust, or chaff, if nothing else is available. With a tight lid and a wet cloth spread over the top, water will keep ice cold in this arrangement.

WATER COOLER

The uses of such a cooler may be multiplied to include keeping many things cool in the house.

## KEEP FOOD COOL IN SUMMER

A very convenient and serviceable place to keep dairy products may be formed by sinking a large barrel in the ground. A shady spot should be chosen, or the heat of the sun will affect the temperature. Fill in around the barrel with small stones, gravel and sand, dampened in order to maintain coolness.

Construct a box around and above the top of the barrel, and bank up with solid earth, preferably

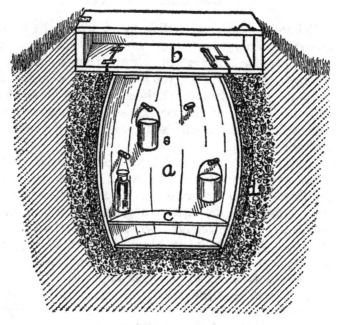

FOOD COOLER

clay. This drains off the water when it rains. It also makes the bottom of the barrel farther down from the top of the opening, which further promotes coolness. Next shape a light, inner lid to place on top of the barrel, and then make a strong, hinged lid for the box, and arrange it so it may be fastened down tightly.

Sprinkle a little dampened sand on the bottom of the barrel, and your little barrel cellar is ready for use. By being careful several vessels may be arranged one above the other in this handy little receptacle. Air out occasionally to prevent mold and odors from collecting.

## A COOLER DUMMY

Where a deep, cool well is located near the house an arrangement may be devised that will serve the purpose of a refrigerator. Construct a frame of strong boards with a groove in which a board on the side of the box of shelves can run. Attach a rope to the top of the box of shelves, pass it over a wheel on the crank shaft and balance with a counter weight.

If the frame is 16 feet long and extended down near to the surface of the water the lowest temperature may be secured. A nice looking top may be constructed for the arrangement, with a door opening into the shelves when they are drawn to the top. Most wells are almost as cool as a refrigerator, and this sort of an arrangement serves the purpose with a great deal less expense.

A wire clothesline will serve as a cable. Any old pieces of iron will do for the counter weight, and it is well to have a ratchet wheel, such as are found on old chain pumps, to prevent the elevator dropping when it is well filled. Make as many parts as possible of wood to prevent rusting. One such elevator is 42 inches high and 18 inches square.

------------

Turning the grindstone is hard work; but if you use it as a muscle developer it will help out.

## AN OUTDOOR CLOSET

When the housewife has baked a pie or a pudding for dinner and wishes to cool it quickly in winter it has to be set out of doors; but there the trouble begins. It cannot be set upon the snow, since that would melt and engulf the hot dish. Moreover, the cat or dog, or some neighbor's cat or dog, is likely to be lurking about the door, ready for pie. Let the handy man make a little out-of-door cupboard for the use of the housekeeper, locating it beside the kitchen door. Get an empty grocery box of the right size and hinge the cover to the top, placing a knob on the other edge. Make a support for this closet by driving two strips of wood into the ground and screwing two crosswise strips of board to the tops. Lay the grocery box on its side on these supports and nail it to them from the inside.

Here anything hot can be placed to cool quickly, and with the cover down there will be no danger from cats or dogs or hens. If desired to give a freer access to the cold air, several holes can be bored in each end and in the bottom before putting the box in position on the supports. If the ground is frozen too hard to insert the strips of board, the closet can be placed against the side of the house, close to the kitchen door, and supported in place by two wooden brackets. Another plan to secure the same result would be to make the closet and screw a wooden handle to the middle of the top, with holes bored in ends and back. When it is to be used put the dish, or dishes, inside and set the closet out onto the snow beside the door.

Taste the joy
That springs from labor.—Longfellow.

## HOMEMADE REFRIGERATOR

Take two large boxes, one 2 inches smaller than the other every way, and bore two 1-inch holes in the bottom of each box for drainage. Fill up 2 inches in the large box with powdered charcoal or coal ashes. Put the smaller box inside and fill the space all around with the charcoal or ashes. Fix the lids to both boxes to fit tightly. Put shelves on both sides of inner box. Leave a place in the center of the box of ice. A rack, made of lath, can be laid at the bottom for ice to rest on.

## ICELESS BUTTER AND MILK COOLER

The accompanying picture shows how a well may be utilized during the warm months for cooling

butter, milk and other perishable articles. It will be found very handy as a substitute for a refrigerator when the farmer has no ice supply. Anyone can make a triangular-shaped frame for the windlass, which is placed above the well; and anyone can also put the trap doors in the platform of the well. These doors should be pro-

COLD STORAGE FOR MILK

vided with a lock, so children cannot fall in. A pin may be placed on the handle side of the windlass to prevent the crank from turning around when the box is lowered to the desired depth.

The picture is only suggestive. The shape and size of the various parts will depend upon the style of the well. Preferably, the box should be made of galvanized iron and have perforations in the bottom, so it may be lowered right into the water. Of course, this would not be feasible if the materials to be kept cold were not first placed in sealed receptacles. Where a well with a bucket pump or the ordinary wooden pump is the only available place to put such a cooler, the cooler may be at one side of the well. If necessary, the position of the pump may be shifted.

---

Knowledge is of two kinds. We know a subject ourselves, or we know where we can find information upon it.—Samuel Johnson.

Every addition to true knowledge is an addition to human power.—Horace Mann.

But now my task is smoothly done,
I can fly, or I can run.—Milton.

---

## A VENTILATED PUMP PLATFORM

Here is a way to keep the well clean and pure at all times. Make the frame of the platform of 2 x 4's, allowing a space 2 to 6 inches between the top and bottom parts of the sides. This space is covered on the inside with a fly screen to keep out dirt and insects, and outside of this with a larger meshed screen to keep out large vermin. This gives good ventilation to the well, which never becomes foul. In the winter cover the platform with straw and snow.

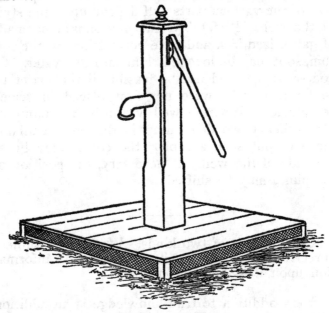

HELPS TO KEEP WATER PURE

## CLEANING A WELL

To remove floating litter from a well, take an ordinary sand sieve, and, after marking off the rim into three parts, attach a wire to any of the two points and to this improvised handle attach a rope. Fasten the end of the rope to the third point in the rim and a weight to the sieve, so that it can be lowered into the well and will sink. When used, sink the sieve edgewise into the water and pull the rope with a single attachment and it may be lifted out with all the floating sticks and timber on the surface of the water.

## DOG POWER FOR PUMP

This sketch shows an arrangement for making use of the dog for carrying water. It simply consists of a wheel 8 feet in diameter and 18 inches

DOG POWER PUMPING DEVICE

wide, with room enough inside for the dog to walk around, where he acts as a tread power, which causes the pump to revolve. In southern California there are a number of these dog-power pumps, which cost less than $15. A good-sized dog can easily earn his living in an arrangement of this kind.

## FILTER FOR CISTERN WATER

The problem of keeping water in a cistern clean is most easily solved by not allowing it to get dirty, as can be done by the device shown in the drawing on page 69. Two barrels, each with a perforated false bottom, are set side by side beneath the water spout from the roof and connected with a pipe leading to the cistern. Above the false bottoms fine gravel and then sand are packed to the depth of 8 or more inches. On top of the sand rest stout floats as large as can be let down into the barrels. From near the margin of the floats two heavy wires extend vertically upward about 2 feet to engage loosely near their centers with a tilting spout by means of knobs on both the ends of the spout and the wires.

When the barrels are empty the floats rest on the sand. As the water begins to pour in one barrel it strikes the float, but is prevented from gouging a very deep hole at the outside of the barrel by striking a strip of wood about 1 inch high, 2 inches wide and 1 foot long. This spreads the flow. A layer of gravel at this place would also help prevent gouging. If the flow is too great to filter away readily, the float will rise and the knob on the wire will engage with the spout, which will be tilted until the flow will suddenly start into the other barrel. If the delivery pipe to the cistern be large enough there should be no danger of either barrel overflowing. When the sand becomes dirty a few minutes will serve to remove it and put in fresh. This will insure clean water in the cistern, and greatly reduce the number of times the disagreeable job of cleaning out the cistern must be done.

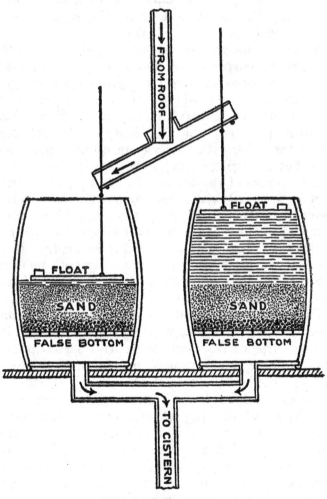

TWO-BARREL FILTER

## A HANDY WATER FILTER

Nearly every farm can boast of good water, but no water, either from well, spring or stream, is pure, as it all contains more or less animal or vegetable matter. The only way to make it pure is to filter it, just as is done in city supply reservoirs, or private filtering tanks.

A simple water filter is very easily made that answers all purposes for domestic use. The plan of its operations is identical with that employed in large reservoirs where water is filtered on a large scale for general distribution. This filter consists, primarily, of two flower pots, set one above the other. In the bottom of the upper pot is stuffed a large sponge. A sponge is also stuffed in the bottom of the lower pot, but it is more adequately supplied with filtering material by placing above the sponge a layer of smooth pebbles, then a layer of coarse sand, and still above this a layer of pounded charcoal 3 or 4 inches in depth. It is also best to place another layer of smooth pebbles above the charcoal, to prevent it from being stirred up during the circulation of the water.

The upper pot should be the largest, and if the lower one is strong, the upper one may stand in it, or two strips of wood will serve as a base support. The two pots thus arranged are placed on a three-legged stool with a hole in it, through which the water drips through the bottom of the lower pot into the mouth of a jug set underneath. The upper pot serves as a reservoir, and its sponge stops the coarser impurities, and thus the filtering layers of the lower one may be used for a year without being renewed, though it is necessary frequently to clean the sponge of the upper pot.

The layers of sand and charcoal of the lower pot are positively effective in stopping all animal and vegetable matter, as well as many smaller impurities in the water. The only trouble one may experience with it is in neglecting the upper sponge for too long a time, or in stuffing it in too loosely, thus allowing the water to pass from the upper pot faster than it can filter through the lower one. Only a little attention, once or twice a month, is sufficient to keep this simple filter in perfect running order.

## DELIVERING MAIL BY TROLLEY

Where the house stands some distance back from the highway a trolley can be rigged up to save steps in getting the mail. The box is hung on two pulley door hangers, as shown in cut. A strong post, with a bent arm, is set next the highway, *a*, suspended between it and the house, on which the box runs. A pulley is fastened in or to, the post, and over it runs a

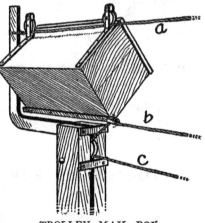

TROLLEY MAIL BOX

cord, *b*, *c*, to pull the box back and forth between the house and the road. The box is sent down to meet the carrier, who places the mail in it, and then it is quickly pulled back to the house.

## BEAUTY IN A BARREL

A very nice ornamentation for the lawn is shown in the picture.  It is made by sawing an oil barrel in two as shown, and mounting it on legs.  Paint it and set one-half of the barrel on each side of the walk and use them for growing flowers in during the summer.  Care should be taken to have the hoops thoroughly nailed to the staves and to have the heads solid.  Dark green or dark red are good colors for the painting.  If preferred, the barrel may rest upon the ground, but should be securely braced or blocked to prevent rolling.

HALF-BARREL PLANT HOLDER

## STORAGE BIN FOR VEGETABLES

Instead of keeping the vegetables in barrels or boxes scattered all over the cellar, have a set of storage bins.  Take six drygoods boxes and bolt them together as shown in the drawing.  Put legs on them to hold them off the floor and a cover on the top.  Then paint on the boxes the names of the vegetables. It is most convenient to have the vegetables most frequently used in the upper boxes, which would not be true of the bin shown in the picture. If the upper row of boxes is attached to each other, but not to the lower ones, the top section can easily be moved enough to make filling the lower boxes a simple matter. Otherwise, the vegetables

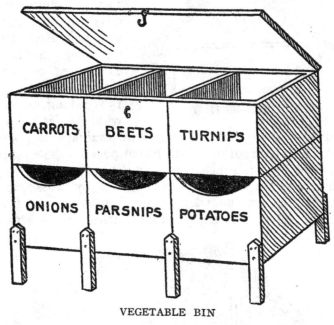

CARROTS    BEETS    TURNIPS

ONIONS    PARSNIPS    POTATOES

VEGETABLE BIN

would have to be put in through the openings at the top of each box a few at a time by hand, instead of pouring them in.

Many people would not care to keep their potatoes in such a sectional bin, preferring a large separate bin. It certainly is all right for other root vegetables, and many other products of the farm that are stored might well be kept handy for use in such a labeled sectional bin.

## AN INEXPENSIVE CELLAR

A temporary cellar is sometimes necessary in cold countries where that under the house is not

CROSS-SECTION

sufficient for storing vegetables. A very effective and u s e f u l temporary cellar may be constructed after the following method, as shown by the drawings: Dig a pit 15 feet long, 10 feet wide, 4 feet deep in a solid, dry place where the drainage is good. Put a gable roof of 1-inch board over the hole, supported by 2 x 4-inch strips at the eaves, gable and half way up the sides. Strengthen by crossbeams and a central support if the lumber is not first class. Over this place 8 to 10 inches of dry straw

TEMPORARY CELLAR

well packed and over the entire structure, excepting one end, pack earth 12 to 14 inches deep. The surface should be smooth to shed water. It is better if plastered with mud covered with sods.

The door end must be double-walled and the space filled with straw.  The door must also be double and its margin packed with cloth strips, so as to be practically airtight.  If possible, the pit should be drained by a tile, the end of which is covered with a piece of wire netting to prevent the entrance of rodents.  Such a cellar will prevent freezing during usual winter weather.  The door should be opened on mild days and the interior aired thoroughly.  The size and depth of the pit may be varied according to needs.

## CLOTHESLINE UP AND DOWN

Heavy posts should be set for the ends, 3 feet in and 3 feet out of the ground.  It is not necessary for the center post to be as heavy as the end ones. Have the posts clean and smooth, so they will not soil the clothes when blown against them.  Take a

ELEVATED CLOTHESLINE

piece of 2 x 4-inch hard wood 5 feet long for the lever.  Fasten to the post near the top with a 3/4-inch bolt, 2 feet next to the line and 3 feet for the lever.  A block holds the lever in position while the clothes are being put on.  A button holds the lever upright when the line is hoisted.

# A CLOTHES HORSE

There is no little thing that will save the household so much as a revolving clothes horse, so near the back stoop that the clothes may be hung on it without stepping out in the snow. A solid post should have a hole bored in the top and the arms may be beveled and spiked to a piece of plank through which a bolt passes into the post, or each arm may be bored to let the bolt pass through it. Three, four or five arms may be used as desired, and of any length, provided all are of one length. No skill is required in making it, as the rope holds the arms up simply by being tight enough. It is well to set the post before measuring for the arms, so that they may be sure to reach the veranda. Some laths may be nailed together at first to make a model, if you are not sure of your ability as a carpenter.

# A TOILET CLOSET

A small closet in a home, for keeping medicines and toilet articles, is a great convenience. One consists of ½-inch pine, 4 inches wide, planed and put together so as to be 2 x 3 feet. It has four shelves. The door is of thin pine, free from knots, planed, hinged and with a back catch. The outside of frame and door is varnished. Being in the toilet room, it is indeed a very useful as well as ornamental piece of furniture. It has no back casing or boards; simply rests against the wall. It is held in place by four short pieces of band iron, one end of each band being fastened to back of frame, the other end fastened to the wall by a screw. All kinds of medicines, shaving materials, soaps, wash rags, can there be kept.  If there is no other looking-glass in the room, one may be fastened on the outside of door.

## REVOLVING CELLAR SHELF

A handy cellar shelf that will save the house-keeper many steps may be arranged at the side of the cellar stairs, within easy reach upon descending a few steps.  The shelf is contrived from an old axle and wheel.  The axle is fastened to hang from the nearest beam to the stairway.  The wheel is covered with thin, smoothly planed boards and the axle is kept well oiled, so the wheel will revolve readily, bringing all parts of the shelf within reach at need.

## WATER SUPPLY FOR FARMHOUSE

Farmers can have running water, hot or cold, in their dwelling houses at a cost of fifty dollars and up, depending upon the size of the house and the kind of equipment needed.  This makes possible the bath and toilet room, protection from fire, the easy washing of windows and walks, the sprinkling of lawns, the irrigating of gardens, and all the other conveniences which a few years ago were thought possible only in cities, where big water systems were available.  This is one of the things that makes farm life attractive.  It lessens the work in the house, insures a fine lawn and garden, reduces danger from fire, adds greatly to comfort and convenience in every direction.

The way to secure this is to install a water supply system, with a pressure tank in the basement.

This pressure tank is so arranged that by pumping it full under strong air pressure the water is forced all over the house, and is available for the bathroom, toilet room and the garden or fire hose. The water is distributed about the house exactly as it is in city homes, by means of galvanized iron pipes. Where a small building is to be supplied and the

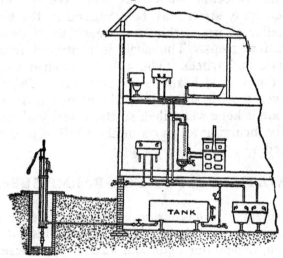

HOUSE WATER SYSTEM

amount of water to be used is not large, the system can be installed for $50. For the average house $90 is a better figure. Where the house is large, and where considerable amounts of water are needed for the lawn and garden, and possibly also for washing carriages, automobiles and horses, a larger system should be installed, costing up to $150.

## Installation and Operation

Its installation is easy, and its operation is exceedingly simple. Any pipe fitter or plumber can put in the plant so that it will work perfectly. All that is needed for operating is to keep the tank pressure up to the desired point. This may be 20, 40, 60 or 100 pounds. A few strokes of the pump, if the work is done by hand, is sufficient. If a lot of water is used, of course the amount of pumping will increase. By being economical in the use of water, that is to say, wasting none, this matter of pumping is not at all a serious problem.

The most satisfactory method of pumping, however, is to use a windmill, or what is much better, a gasoline engine. Every up-to-date farm ought to have a small gasoline engine, which can be utilized not only for operating this water supply system, but for churning, sawing wood, cutting feed and doing a dozen and one other jobs about the farm. It would take only a few minutes of pumping to raise the pressure in the tank the desired height. With the engine it will not be necessary to be economical in using water, provided the well is a good one, and the supply of water large.

### Experience with Water Supply System

C. A. Shamel of Illinois, editor of the Orange Judd Farmer, has a system of this kind in his country home. It cost $75. He put in a bathroom, a toilet, has a hot water tank in connection with the kitchen range, and no money ever expended on that farm has given anything like the amount of satisfaction and comfort as that paid for this water supply system. Arrangement is made to take care of the waste water and sewage by running a large tile from the bathroom, one-quarter of a mile distant, to a large cistern, located in the center of a big field. This is disinfected about

twice a year, and is easily handled. There is never
any trouble with the water pipes, even during the
coldest weather. Neither has there been any difficulty with the waste system. In fact, the water
supply is practically perfect, and the people on that
farm don't see how any farmer who can get together $75 or $100 can afford to be without it.

Up to date all the pumping has been done by
hand. With the pump in perfect condition, this is
not a laborious problem. On two occasions the
pump valve became slightly defective through
wear, and it was not convenient to fix it for a few
weeks, being somewhat distant from the factory.
With this condition it required a great deal more
labor to do the pumping, but even with this dis-
advantage, it was not a serious proposition.

The illustration indicates the arrangement of a
water supply system, and, as can be readily seen,
it is very simple. Notice the hand force pump tank
in the basement to hold the water under pressure,
and the arrangement of lavatories, bath and kitchen
hot water service. The system can also be used
for supplying water to stock tanks, and these may
be located anywhere on the farm. The pressure
developed in the tank is sufficient to force the water
anywhere wanted. This use will, of course, depend
entirely upon the wishes of the owner and is simply
a matter of cost of pipes. It can very readily be
used for delivering water to dairy or other stock
barns, where it can be run into water troughs in the
stalls, or elsewhere, as desired.

## WARNING AGAINST FIRE

A handy device that will give an alarm in case
the roof catches fire close to the chimney is shown

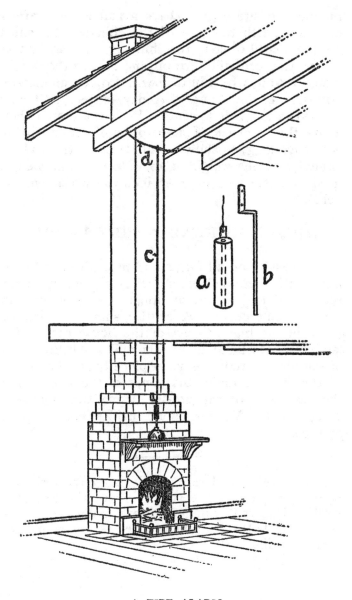

A FIRE ALARM

on the opposite page. Drive a nail in two rafters
on a line with the face of the chimney, to which
stretch a cord close to the chimney, so that, in case
of fire, the cord will burn off and release the weight
hanging to it, which in turn will drop on an electric
button and ring a bell. A dry battery will cost
20 cents and a bell 50 cents. Place these on a shelf
above the fireplace. Place a piece of heavy wire, $b$,
10 inches long, as shown, and fasten to the wall or
chimney for the weight, $a$, to slide on. The weight
need be suspended only an inch or two above the
bell.

## WHERE TO HANG A FIRE LADDER

A necessity on all farms and near all farm buildings are ladders and other means of getting on the
roofs, and in and out of upper story windows in
time of emergency. A scuttle should be left or
made in the highest part of the house roof and a
ladder should be at hand that will reach the eaves
of the highest roof. A good place to store a ladder
of this kind is under the eaves of the L or along
the rear wall of the house. Have two hooks to
hang it on. Make a good ladder and keep it
painted.

If your cellar is dark, there is danger of accidents
when going down the stairs. Have the last step
whitened so that you may easily know when you
are at the bottom. You can see this step plainly
even in a dim light.

## A HANDY FEED BASKET

P ROVIDE a feed basket like this to strap upon the nose of a horse when giving the animal feed while away from the stable. It is simpler to make than the round basket, and has an added advantage. When not in use, the two sides press to-gether and occupy scarcely any room. Cut out two semi-circular pieces of wood from a ¾-inch board in the shape suggested in the cut. Setting them at the proper distance apart, tack a strip of canvas, or other stout cloth, around the curved partition, as shown in the accompany-ing picture. Nail a strap and a buckle at the sides, to go over the head, and the feed basket will be complete.

FEED BASKET

The form of this basket more nearly fits the shape of a horse's head, and be-sides, because of its oblong shape, gives the horse more freedom in opening his mouth than does the close-fitting round basket.

---

He who will not be counseled cannot be helped.

## MAKE THE HORSE EAT SLOWLY

If your horse has the habit of bolting his feed you
can easily remedy it by making a self-feeder on his
box. The accompanying drawing
shows how a feeder may be made
similar to a poultry feed hopper.
The contrivance may be made of
inch boards large enough to hold
one feed. The horse can get the
grain only in small quantities and
so cannot eat it more rapidly than
he should. The bottom must be made with enough
slant to insure all of the feed coming out in the
trough.

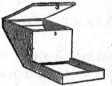

HOLDS ONE FEED

---

I am only one,
But I am one.
I cannot do everything,
But I can do something.
What I can do I ought to do;
And what I ought to do
By the grace of God I will do.

---

## STALLS BETTER THAN STANCHIONS

The only point in favor of stanchions is that they
take up less room than stalls, but the increase in
milk is a reward for allowing more space and convenience to each cow. The cut shows one kind of
stall. The rack, a, is of hardwood 30 inches high,
with the slats wide enough so the cow can thrust
her nose through up to her eyes.

The bottom of the rack is 18 inches wide, extending into the stall toward the cow. The feed

box, *b*, slides through an opening in the stall on the barn floor. It can be drawn into the feedway, cleansed out and a new feed put in without being disturbed by the cow. The halter strap, *c*, is just long enough to allow the cow to lie down comfortably. The gutter, *d*, is 8 inches lower than the

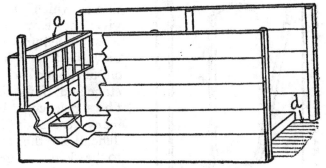

PLAN OF COW STALL

stall floor. When she lies down she will put her head under the rack in kneeling and when she gets up, she will move backward so that she can look through the rack. The length and width of stall can be made to suit the cows. Small breeds, like Jerseys and Ayrshires, will need about 6 inches less each way than Holsteins and Shorthorns.

Knowledge is proud that he has learned so much;
Wisdom is humble that he knows no more.
—Cowper.

The man who is always poking his nose into other folks' business rarely has any of his own worth attending to.

There is no knowledge that is not power.—Emerson.

## GOOD TIES FOR COWS

The merits of stanchions and other forms of cow ties have been debated by dairymen for a long time.

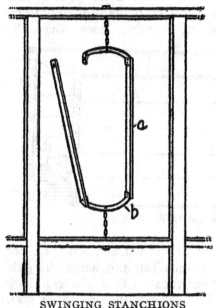

SWINGING STANCHIONS

The mass of experience is in favor of the tying arrangement which will give the cow the most freedom of movement. T h e old-fashioned solid stanchion fails in t h i s respect. In many cases it is difficult for the cow to lie down or get up with her head fast in one of these stanchions.

The heavy swinging stanchions have advantages o v e r this, but it also must be criticised in many cases, because of its weight and of the consequent lack of freedom on the part of the cow. A very light swinging stanchion is the best type of that form. It is easy to fasten, as the cows will in most cases put their heads in position as they go into the stall. There is not so much danger of the dairyman being struck by the horns of the cow in fastening these stanchions. Many modern barns are equipped with this kind.

The chain tie is favored in many sections. This consists simply of a crosschain with considerable slack, attached to a ring at each end which runs over a perpendicular iron rod about 18

inches long. In the
center of this chain
is a loop with a snap
which goes around
the cow's neck. This
arrangement g i v e s
the greatest free-
dom, and allows the
cow to lie down and
get up without dif-
ficulty. If light par-
titions are used be-
tween the heads of
the cows no difficulty
will be experienced
in their s t r i k i n g
each other with their
horns. This is by

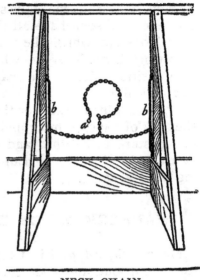

NECK CHAIN

far the least expensive of cow ties, and is at the
same time one of the most satisfactory.

## HANDY CALF-FEEDING DEVICE

To feed a half-dozen calves at once is entirely
possible if one uses the device shown here. A man

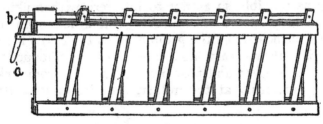

STANCHIONS FOR CALVES

who has one reports no more trouble with calves
since he has used this. He rattles a couple of

buckets together, the calves come running up to the fence and soon have all their heads through the stanchions, to which they are easily fastened by throwing down lever, *a*, which draws the bar, *b*, into position.  Then one may feed each calf without difficulty.

Leave a 4-inch space for the calves' heads.  Make the rack of 1-inch lumber and it can be moved from one pasture to another and attached to the fence or a couple of posts.  It can also be used for holding ewes at lambing time.

## MANAGEMENT OF KICKING COWS

Make a slatted stall just high enough so the cow can't jump out, and wide enough to hold her comfortably, with nothing to spare, and narrower at the end, where her feed box should be placed as high from the ground as is comfortable for her to eat out of.  This slatted stall should be long enough to have cleats through which a bar or two should be run behind the cow to keep her from backing out, and also places to run a bar in front of her hind legs about the hock joint, or as high up as possible so as not to interfere with milking. A hole about 18 or 20 inches wide is left open for this purpose from the ground up to the cow's flank, which allows easy and safe access to the udder, while the cleat and post prevent the cow from kicking outwardly at the milker, thus insuring safety.

## A HANDY MILKING STOOL

Milkers who have trouble with restless cows that invariably either upset the pail or get a quantity of

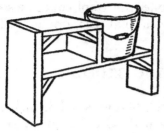

STOOL TO HOLD PAIL

dirt in it will find the stool shown here a remedy for their troubles. It is also very serviceable in fly time. The upright pieces forming the legs and ends of stools are made of 2 x 8-inch pieces about 1 foot long. The supports for the bucket and the seat are made of inch boards. To secure rigidity it is well to put three-cornered blocks under the seat and bucket board as brace stays. The most restless cow is not likely to upset the bucket from this stool.

## THE EVER READY STOOL

A very convenient stool for use in milking the cow in yard or field is shown in the cut. It is merely a one-legged stool to which is attached four straps connecting with a broad strap that is buckled around the waist. The stool is quickly fastened to the milker and is always in a position so one can sit down anywhere. Such a stool with a short leg would also be useful in the garden. Of course, if one pre-

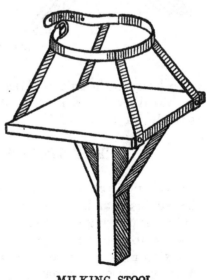

MILKING STOOL

ferred four legs instead of one, the stool could be so made, but experience proves that the one-legged kind serves well.

## CHEAP MILKING STOOL

A cheap and very useful milking stool is made of the reel from which barbed wire has been removed. Saw off the ends so it will set level and

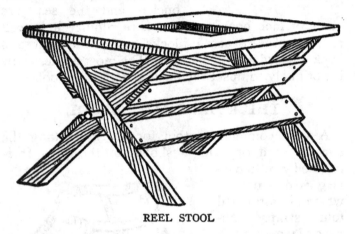

REEL STOOL

cut a board to fit on top. Make a hand hole through the board as shown in the illustration and the stool is ready for use.

## KEEP STOOLS CLEAN

Much milk contamination is undoubtedly due to the careless handling of the milk stools. When the milker is through milking one cow he gives the stool a toss, then he picks it up again when he starts to milk the next cow and his hands become more or less contaminated from the stool and from them the dirt drops into the milk pail during the milking.

When the milking is over, the stool is left in the yard or on the barn floor. It is so easy to make a small rack and to bore holes in the legs of the

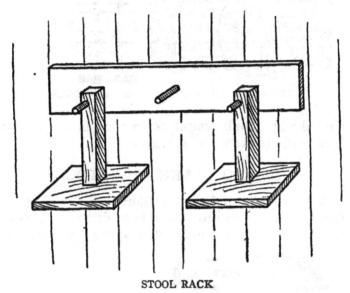

STOOL RACK

stool, so that they may be hung up. This keeps them out of the dirt and it is only necessary to brush them off carefully once in a while to keep them scrupulously clean.

---

The man who is constantly changing his mind usually has little to change.

---

## A USEFUL STOCK CART

Here is a handy transfer cart, made with wheels and crossarch of an old corn plow to carry a hog

or sheep, pigs or a calf.   Raise the tongue, which
lets the rear end on ground, then drive in the animal,

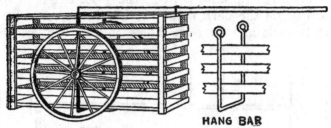

HANG BAR

TRANSFER CART FOR SMALL ANIMALS

shut the gate, pull tongue down and you have your
load ready to fasten to a wagon.

## HOW TO STAKE OUT STOCK

A convenient and simple contrivance so that no
harm can come to the animal is to drive two stakes
several feet apart and stretch a rope or wire on

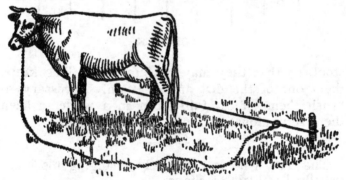

COW TIED OUT TO FEED

which a ring is placed.   To this ring fasten halter
strap.   The animal can graze up and down on both
sides without tangle or injury.   The ring slides,
and the stretched wire will give some.

## FEED BOX FOR FIELD

A handy feed box for use in open lots or when steers are being fed upon grass is shown in the

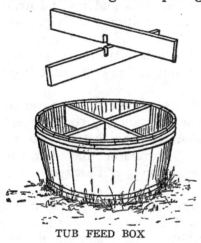

cut. Cut a barrel in two and strengthen the halves by placing a frame of two b o a r d s across the inside, as shown in this sketch. T h i s will prevent the tub being smashed and w i l l a l l o w four animals to eat out of the trough without bothering each other unnecessarily. It is important that a very strong barrel be selected and that the hoops be nailed to each stave.

TUB FEED BOX

---

Be advis'd;
Heat not a furnace for your foe so hot
That it do singe yourself: we may outrun,
By violent swiftness, that which we run at,
And lose by over-running.—Henry VIII.

Have more than thou showest,
Speak less than thou knowest,
Lend less than thou owest,
Ride more than thou goest,
Learn more than thou trowest,
Set less than thou throwest.—King Lear.

Use or practice of a thing is the best master.

## CHEAP SHEDS OF STRAW

It would pay every farmer to put up in the pastures some kind of protection for his sheep, hogs and cattle. Where labor is scarce and hay and straw is plentiful and cheap, a condition which prevails in many large sections, straw sheds and barns are very profitable. Put up a framework of posts 8 feet high, 16 feet wide and as long as needed; 30 feet is a good length.

The posts are hewed evenly on two sides and set so that a bale of straw will fit snugly between them. They are cut off at a uniform height and a 2 x 6 spiked securely on top. Rafters are nailed to this and covered loosely with poles. Baled straw is used for the sides.

After the sides are up the roof is covered 2 feet deep with loose straw held in place with a few poles that are tied together in pairs and placed over the ridge. Several of these sheds have been built for five years and have not needed any attention.

———

Life is made up not of great sacrifices or duties, but of little things, in which smiles and kindness, and small obligations given habitually, are what win and preserve the heart and secure comfort.— Sir H. Davy.

You must cut your coat according to your cloth.

———

## FEED TROUGH FOR SHEEP

For a sheep trough procure two 6-inch boards, *a*, about 3 feet long and at the bottom of each fasten another board, *b*. Make a flat trough and let the

ends project above the top. Bore a hole through
each end and also through the standards, *a*, and
hang the trough on bolts. After the sheep eat and

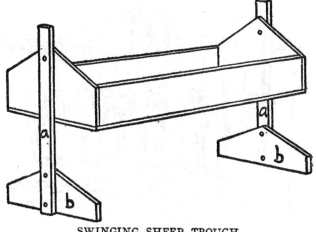

SWINGING SHEEP TROUGH

leave the cobs, or if it rains, the trough can be
turned bottom side up and quickly cleaned.

———

The luck that I believe in
   Is that which comes with work,
And no one ever finds it
   Who's content to wish and shirk.
The men the world calls lucky
   Will tell you, every one,
That success comes, not by wishing,
   But by hard work, bravely done.

———

## A NOVEL FEED RACK

An overhead manger, as shown in the sketch,
is excellent for sheep or calves. It should hang
just high enough so that they will pass under with-

out rubbing their backs. When filled with hay from above they will eat of it at their pleasure, and at the same time it will not take up floor space.

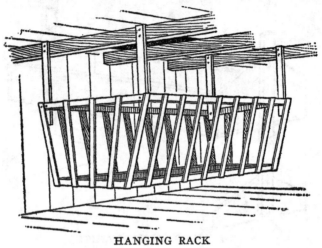

HANGING RACK

Such a manger is not suitable for grains or fine cut fodders, as too much may be wasted.

## A WHEELBARROW SHEEP TROUGH

It very often happens that one wishes to run the sheep on several different pastures during the

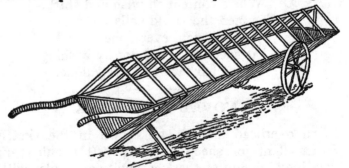

PORTABLE RACK FEEDER

season. If heavy feed racks are used it is quite a task to move them. The drawing shows a rack that can be easily moved from one field to another by one person. It is simply mounted upon a pair of wheels and has handles on the other end.

If the rack is made very large, it can be easily attached to a wagon, and thus drawn from place to place. The one shown is mounted on old cultivator wheels.

## PACKING THE FLEECE

One of the best ways to pack a fleece is to lay it upon a table, turn in the head and tail, then the

FLEECE TYING BOX

flanks. After this roll it up into a neat roll and tie firmly, using such a device as here illustrated.

The tying box is made from light lumber with slots, as shown, through which the rope is passed. The fleece is placed upon this rope and the roll easily tied. Wool buyers prefer to have the fleece loose, light to handle and elastic and tied up so that it can be opened if needed.

## EASY TO HANDLE HEAVY HOGS

The old fashion of having a lot of help around at hog-killing time is going out, owing to the use of better appliances for handling the animals after killing. You may rig up a simple arrangement so

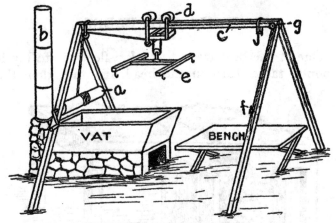

ONE-MAN BUTCHERING RIG

that you can handle heavy hogs without assistance. Build a fire box with a flue, *b*, of three joints of old stovepipe. The vat is made of heavy galvanized iron 4 feet long by 2 feet wide and 18 inches deep.

Over this erect a frame of 2 x 4-inch strips, upon which place an old traveler from a hay carrier, or construct one similar to *d*. With the windlass arrangement, *a*, and the tackle, *e*, to which are attached the four feet of the hog, you can convey it from the vat to the bench. A rope, *c*, passing over the pulley at *g*, serves to pull the carrier, *d*, over the bench from the vat.

# HEATING WATER FOR HOG KILLING

A device which is superior to the old iron kettle for heating water is shown in this sketch. Take a piece of 2-inch iron pipe 8 feet long and have it securely screwed into the bottom of a stout vinegar barrel. In the other end of the pipe screw a large wooden block.

SIMPLE WATER BOILER

By arranging the affair as shown in the sketch water in the barrel will be heated rapidly and can be removed as desired without bothering the fire. Do not make the mistake of putting a metal cap on the end of the pipe, or the steam may sometimes burst the piping before the cap will come off. The wooden block acts as a safety valve and will fly out if pressure is too great.

# A FARM SLAUGHTERHOUSE

If one butchers his own stock on the farm he would do well to fix up a small building for a slaughterhouse. This can be done so easily and at such small expense that almost any farmer can afford one. It is generally most convenient to have it near the hog yard, for then the refuse can be easily conveyed to the hogs. Indeed it would not be a half bad idea to have it in some instances a part of the hog house. The room in which to kill

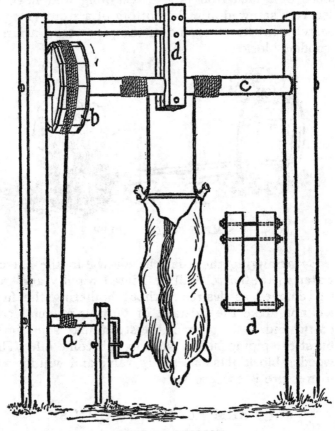

CARCASS DERRICK

cattle and hogs should not be less than 15 feet square. This will give plenty of space for the work. As much of the room should be kept clear from fixtures as possible.

The floor should be made of concrete graded
so that it will all drain to a central opening. A
pipe should carry the liquid from this opening to a
trough in the hog yard. The ideal way would be
to make the walls of concrete for about 3 feet from
the ground. This will make it much easier to keep
the place clean. It is quite necessary that a good
supply of water be close at hand. If possible, a
water pipe with hose attached should be in the
house. This will enable one to flood the floor at
any time.

On page 99 is a picture of a very good device
for handling the carcasses. It is made of a heavy
roller, *c*, 5 to 6 inches thick, and long enough to
reach across the width of the room. It is supported in the middle by a bracket, *d*, detail of which
is shown in the drawing. This makes it possible
to lift a carcass of any weight. A drum, *b*, is attached to the roller at one end, over which is run
the rope that communicates with the crank, *a*, at
the floor. Any man handy with tools can make
this derrick.

In order to simplify matters one may use a barrel
cart water heater. This barrel has a valve attached
at the bottom. To this is fastened a rubber hose
that communicates with a small coil of pipes. This
coil of pipes in turn communicates with the top of
the barrel by another rubber hose. The coil of
pipes is placed over a fire built in a hole in the
ground, and the valve is opened.

As soon as the water in the coils becomes hot it
is forced through the rubber hose, and a circulation
is started. This device will heat water very rapidly
and easily. When the water is heated the rubber
hose is detached and the barrel wheeled under the

derrick on which the hog is hung. By means of a crank the carcass is let into the water to be scalded.

With simple devices one man can very easily do the butchering alone. It will be found convenient to have a table that folds up against the side of the building on which to cut up the meat.

## KEEP PIGS OUT OF FEED TROUGH

To prevent hogs crowding and getting in the trough with their feet the accompanying plan will be found practical. You can nail the Vs, or rick-

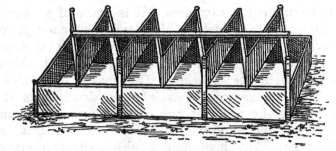

PARTITIONED HOG TROUGH

rack work, on any shaped trough. They fit on a pointed or flat-bottomed trough equally well. Nail a strip lengthwise along the top of the Vs to strengthen them. Stakes driven at intervals and nailed securely to the angles will hold the Vs and trough both solid.

## MOVABLE HOUSE FOR BREEDING SOWS

Individual hog houses may be constructed with four upright walls and a shed roof, as shown below. The walls and the roof are separate and can be easily taken down and replaced. These small

houses can be moved about very easily. The size
of the house will depend upon conditions. The

CONSTRUCTION OF THE HOUSE

construction is shown, so that any farmer with tools
can easily put up one of these houses. With the
individual houses the sow at farrowing time may be
kept alone and away from all disturbance and
there will not be too large a number of pigs in a

THE HOUSE SET UP

small lot if kept in this way. The danger of spreading diseases among the animals is also reduced to a minimum where swine are kept more isolated. When properly bedded and cared for no disastrous disease need be feared. Much depends upon the sanitary conditions.

## WELL-ARRANGED HOG LOTS

An Indiana farmer keeps his pigs in long houses which are divided into compartments opening into small lots. The sketch shows how they stand. Breeding hogs and fattening shotes are allowed the run of their own lots, as well as occasional

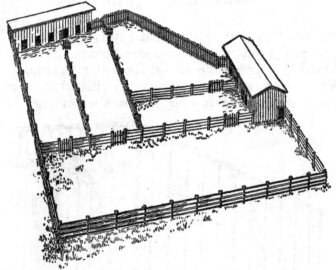

PIG HOUSES AND PENS

changes into the larger field, shown at the bottom of the sketch, which is a timothy and clover pasture. It is better to have pigs in separate quarters in small bunches, for in this way they can be better attended to and the growths are more uniform.

## HANDY PIG CATCHER

Here is a homemade device for catching small pigs which saves much time and annoyance. The net may be made from a discarded lawn tennis net, the rim from a bicycle wheel, and the handle is a heavy rake handle. The net is securely fastened to the rim with some copper wire, while the rim is fastened to the handle with two pieces of band iron. Small pigs caught in the net will not squeal and struggle as when chased around the pen and caught by one leg. The element of excitement is greatly reduced by use of the net, and some would find less fun in the net method. On the whole, however, we recommend it.

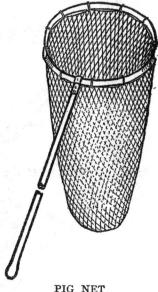

PIG NET

---

The weakest arm is strong enough that strikes with the sword of justice.

Our knowledge is the amassed thought and experience of innumerable minds.—Emerson.

---

## STAIRS FOR THE BARN

A lot of time is saved if one has handy stairs which can be used for throwing down hay as well as a passageway. These steps are made of light material and instead of putting on a lower step, use a block, *c*, and attach the stringers of the stairs to it at each end with a pin. A rope passes over the

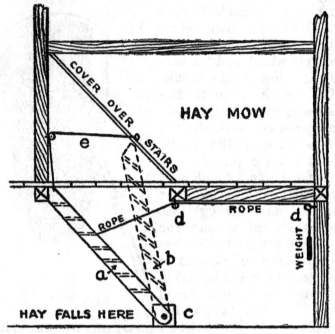

CROSS-SECTION WITH STAIRS

pulleys at *d*, to a weight, which allows the stairway to be held upright while the hay is being put down. The rope, *e*, is handy to pull the stairs into position.

## HANG UP THE LANTERN

Here is a good idea for hanging a lantern over the barn floor. Get two pulleys with screw stems, and screw on in beam over head, the other at top of post. Have a bracket lower on the same post. Take a piece of small but strong cord, and at one end fasten a snap and pass the other end through the pulleys. Put your lantern on the snap and draw it high enough so it will be out of reach of forking hay, and you can see all over the barn floor. You can raise the lantern high enough to pitch hay from the top of the mow with no danger of turning the light over and burning the building and contents.

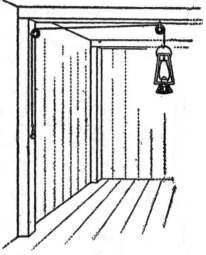

PULLEY-HUNG LANTERN

The end of the cord opposite the lantern m a y b e fastened with a snap, or more length may be allowed for adjusting the height of the lantern, and the cord may be secured by a hitch or a few turns around a button or two spikes driven halfway in and bent over in opposite directions.

## ARRANGEMENT FOR WEIGHING

A homemade balance may be constructed with a joist loosely attached, so as to just balance over the rounded top of a heavy block. It will be useful in weighing hay and other bulky substances for feeding purposes. For weights, use small wooden boxes or bags of stone and sand which have been weighed on other scales. Place the required weight upon the balance and then place feed on the other end until it balances the weight, and it will be accurate enough for all ordinary purposes.

## A BARN WINDLASS

It is easily made of iron pipe or a bar fastened to the ladder or other suitable support by means

WINDLASS

of eyebolts or stout staples, as shown at *a* in the drawing. It may be used for raising grain, wagon boxes and other heavy things to the upper part of the barn, and, if desired, may be rigged with block and falls, so as to increase the power without increasing the effort. A loose bolt placed in a hole will prevent unwinding. The picture shows how simple this device is. Every farmer knows how useful a barn windlass may be.

## GRAIN BOX EASY TO EMPTY

The trouble with most grain boxes is to get out the last third of the grain. Bending over the edge jackknife fashion is neither pleasant nor healthful. A box or bin may be made with half its front on hinges, so that it can be let down and all the contents scooped out without difficulty. The bin may be made from a piano box with a partition in the middle for two kinds of grain.

---

Leave your son a good reputation and an employment.

## EASILY CONSTRUCTED GRAIN BINS

Grain bins with compartments for different kinds of feed are handy in barn or stable. By procuring a number of dry-goods boxes, all of the same size and shape, and nailing them together side by side, so that they will appear as one, the bin is easily made. The cover should extend the entire length of the bin, and though leather hinges will answer, it is better to attach it with iron ones, for then, with a good staple and hasp, the contents can be kept under lock and key if desired.

## A CONVENIENT BARN TRUCK

No dairyman can afford to ignore that which will lighten his labor in any way whatever. Be his stable ever so conveniently constructed, he has enough to do. Hence the importance of his considering a feeding truck or car if he does not have one. Made of good lumber, the only iron about it need be the handle at each end, by which to push or pull it along the feeding alley in front of the cows which are to be fed, and the small trucks on which it is mounted. The wheels procured, any good blacksmith can make these, so that the truck is by no means difficult to construct. The box body should be about 2 feet wide, 20 inches deep and 4½ feet long. Silage can be conveyed in it from the silo to the mangers very readily. If the silo is some distance away, it will save much hard work.

---

If little labor, little are our gaines:
Man's fortunes are according to his paines.
—Herrick.

## TAKES A MAN'S PLACE

In most cases it takes two men to fill a sack of

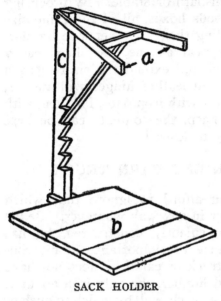

grain, but by using the sack h o l d e r one man can do it alone. M a k e a p l a t f o r m, *b*, 20 inches square, and fasten to it a 2 x 4, *c*, with notches cut in. The arms, *a*, should be 18 inches long. M a k e t h e u p r i g h t piece 3 feet long so that long bags can be h a n d l e d. Some bags will require a still longer upright piece. A device that takes the place of a

SACK HOLDER

man or enables a man to work twice as fast as he could without it is worth while.

———————

A wise old owl sat on an oak,
The longer he stayed the less he spoke.
The less he spoke the more he heard.
Why are not more of us like that wise old bird?

There are but two ways of paying debt: increase of industry in raising income, increase of thrift in laying out.—Carlyle.

If it were done, when 'tis done, then 'twere well
It were done quickly.—Macbeth.

## A HANDY BAG HOLDER

It is constructed with two good boards 1 inch thick and 15 inches wide. The perpendicular one is 3½ feet long, and the horizontal one 2 feet long. These are joined together and braced as shown in the draw-ing, and the hopper is attached, wedged out from the perpendicular board so the bag may wrap it all the way round. The hooks for holding the bag in place can be secured at a hardware store. As the whole affair, if composed of thoroughly seasoned lumber is light to handle, it can easily be carried to any spot where grain is to be put up.

BAG HOLDER

Here is another scheme that saves time and labor and makes it possible for one man to do the work that usually requires two. This one is as good and perhaps better than any device that has been invented in the bag-holder line. In making it, an important point is to attach all parts very securely where they come together, especially the hopper and the braces. Otherwise, with hard usage the holder will get loose and break down.

## A CORN HUSKING RACK

Many who husk their corn by hand find it very tiresome to sit on the floor or ground in a cramped position. A rack made as shown in the drawing

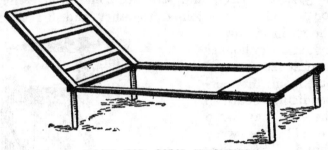

RACK FOR CORN HUSKING

will hold two or three shocks and gives a better place for the husker to sit. Place the stalks crosswise of the bench in front of you.

## A HOMEMADE FEED CUTTER

An old lawn mower can be arranged to make a fairly satisfactory straw or feed cutter. One must

WORKING THE LAWN MOWER

rig up a hopper, as shown in the sketch, and attach the mower to the lower end of it so that the straw or grain will just strike the knives where the grass usually comes into the mower. A crank and a belt arrangement makes it easy for one man to feed and turn the cutter. This is a good use for a lawn mower in the winter time when it is not working outdoors.

## SAW ROOT CUTTER

Those who have cut roots in the winter time with a butcher knife or hatchet will fully appreciate

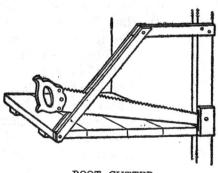

ROOT CUTTER

something better for a root cutter. A Wisconsin farmer has found a serviceable homemade lever cutter very efficient for all roots. For hard ones, like rutabagas, it is about the best thing available. His is made out of an old hand saw, sharpened on the back, fastened by means of a bolt passing through a hole punched at the small end, and held by a guide formed of two pieces of wood secured upright, so as to have a slit for the saw to work in. This contrivance is a success, and with a little practice the roots may be cut very rapidly. See accompanying illustration. The cutter may be mounted upon the wall wherever it will be most convenient. The bench or platform should be at about the height of a common table.

## HOMEMADE CABBAGE CUTTER

A cheap and easily made cabbage and root cutter is shown in the drawing. Take two

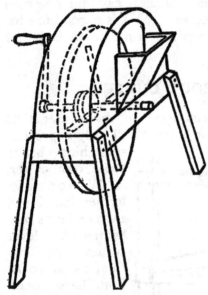

CABBAGE CUTTER

12-inch boards and nail them strongly together. With dividers mark around a circle, then saw out and mark in quarters. Cut four slots 7 inches long on a slant, as shown by dotted lines, so the cabbage will fall through easily. Next cut two circles 4 inches in diameter. Nail one to the large wheel on the back and leave the other loose on the shaft to act as a bearing. Make a frame to admit the wheel, leaving 2 inches clear, and just wide enough so the knives do not strike the side. Make a top over the wheel and put a hopper on the opposite side from the crank. The knives are 8 inches long and can be made from an old bucksaw and ground down sharp, with a bevel on one side. Screw these on the wheel at a slant according to the thickness the cabbage is wanted. A square hole should be cut through the center of the wheel for the shaft.

---

Kindle not the fire that you cannot extinguish.

## A SUBSTANTIAL DRIVEWAY

A plank driveway to the barn is usually made steep in order to save planks. It is continually wearing out and breaking. A substantial driveway with an easy grade can be made by driving down stakes close together on either side, and filling in between with stones, rubbish and earth, packing all down firmly. When full to the top, pack some earth against the outside of the stakes and sod over the sides. This driveway will form an easy rise and will prove very durable.

## FEEDING DRY GROUND GRAIN

 SOME of our friends have found that a poultry feed hopper for feeding ground grain has proved very satisfactory. Make a box 18 x 18 inches and 6 inches deep, then take off one end and fasten to the back with hinges, which forms the cover. Nail a strip, *a*, 3 inches wide across the open side at bottom, which forms the box for the poultry to eat from. Take a board, *b*, the width of inside of box, 14 inches long, and insert in front of box, nailing as shown in cut, with the upper end even with front edge of box and slanting in until a space of 2 inches is left between bottom of board and back of box to allow the feed to pass through.

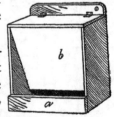

FEED HOPPER

The feed is poured into this hopper and runs down into the box at the bottom as fast as needed. The size of the hopper can be varied to suit the size of the flock. It should be screwed to wall of poultry house about 12 inches from floor. By using this hopper one may keep a dry mixture consisting of wheat bran and middlings and occasionally corn meal, or a small amount of linseed meal, always before the fowls. In addition, some people feed a mixture of whole corn, oats and wheat in the litter morning and evening, also ground green bone and beef scraps.

## KEEPING THE WATER CLEAN

Few drinking fountains are more successful than a large bottle or jug filled with water and inverted. It can be fastened wherever convenient with straps. If a small pan is placed close beneath it the water will flow out as it is used and will remain clean and cool. Place it high enough above the floor of the house so the fowls will not scratch litter into the pan.

## A WATERING RACK FOR HENS

Build a crate of lath 2 feet square, 3 feet high, with a slanting cover to keep the hens off the top. Then tack an 8-inch board in front, level with floor of crate. Nail the rack to post or side of henhouse about 2½ feet from floor, and put your water pan in crate. The hens will quickly learn to fly up and drink by putting corn on the lighting board. T h i s contrivance keeps the hens from spilling their water or scratching dust or chaff into it. Be sure to nail the rack securely to the wall or post where it is put up.

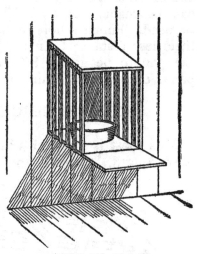

RACK IN PLACE

Keep your shop and your shop will keep you.

## DRINKING FOUNTAIN

The best drinking fountain, in that it is impossible
for small chicks to get drowned, and they cannot
stand in the water
to befoul it, is made
by inverting a can
or pail in a pan a
trifle larger. To-
mato cans with the
edges p o u n d e d
down, leaky pails
with the ears bent
up, in fact anything
with a smooth top
and in which a hole
can be made, can

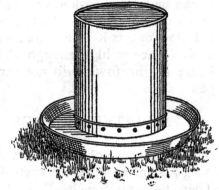

CHICKEN FOUNTAIN

be used. Punch a hole or holes in the side just a
little less distance from the top than the depth of
the pan to be used. Fill with water, invert the
pan over the top, and turn over quickly.

## FOLDING CHICKEN ROOST

This roost is made of 3-inch boards cut any desired length. A small bolt fastens the upright

MOVABLE ROOST

pieces at their top ends, and the horizontal pieces are fastened on with nails. This roost can be kept at any angle, and may be quickly taken out of the house when it is time to clean up. This sort of roost will accommodate more fowls in the same space than the flat kind, but it should not be made very high.

## A GOOD POULTRY NEST

A useful trap nest can be made of grocery boxes. They should be at least 12 inches each way. The illustration shows how they are made. In the cut the trap is set ready for the hen to enter. A cleat, *c*, is fastened to a small piece of cord, which is tied to a nail on the side of the box. Set the trap by raising it and resting the cleat on the nail, with the other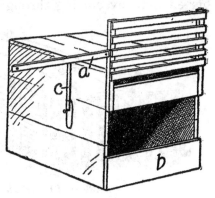

TRAP NEST

end under the arm marked *a*. This leaves an opening from 4 to 6 inches wide, which is not enough for the hen to enter. In going into the nest she will be obliged to raise the trap door, which will let the cleat fall, thus closing the trap after the hen has gone in.

The trap door, the arms and the cleats may be made out of lath. Leave a little space between the boards in the walls, so the heat can escape, otherwise it will be too warm in summer. The bottom board, *b*, in front should be 3 or 4 inches wide, and the lower piece of the trap door should rest against this so the hen cannot get her head through, raise the trap and get out.

## TWO COOPS FROM A BARREL

Very good coops can be made at small cost from empty barrels, as shown in this picture. First, drive shingle nails through the hoops on both sides of each stave and clinch them down on the inside. Then divide the barrel in halves, if it is big enough, by cutting through the hoops and the

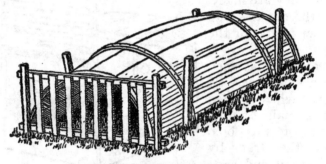

BARREL CHICKEN COOP

bottom. Drive sticks into the ground to hold the coop in place, and drive a long stick at each side of the open end just far enough from coop to allow the front door to be slipped out and in. The night door can be made of the head from the barrel or any solid board, and the slatted door, used to confine the hen, by nailing upright strips of lath to a crosslath at top and bottom.

Weak men wait for opportunities; strong men make them.—Marden.

## A BOX CHICKEN COOP

The diagram shows a convenient way to make a coop for the poultry yard, of which the special feature is its door. Procure a box of the right dimensions and saw a hole, *d*, in one end. Then strengthen the box with narrow strips of wood, *b*, *c*, on each side of the hole *b*, *c*. This acts as a

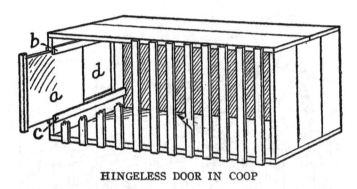

HINGELESS DOOR IN COOP

groove for the door, *a*, to slide in. Thus you have a sliding door, which opens and shuts with the greatest ease. The front of the coop is inclosed with lath, or narrow strips, placed 2½ to 3 inches apart. The top should be covered with a good grade of roofing paper to make it waterproof. A coop of this sort should be 2 to 2½ feet long, 16 inches deep and 2 feet high.

## A LOW POULTRY RUN

A safe and secure run that requires less material than a high pen can be made from laths sawed in two, which would make the sides 2 feet high, making the frame of scantlings and the top of sawed laths, box boards or similar material. The top of the run should consist almost entirely of trap doors, using bits of old harness for hinges, which will look well if cut neatly.  The picture shows one of the doors propped up to show the construction more plainly.  The doors are 4 feet long, the length of a lath, and may be 8 to 10 feet the other way and still not be clumsy, being constructed of such light material.  This trap door is an important feature,

TRAP-DOOR  POULTRY  COOP

as it permits the tender to enter easily for removing top soil and replacing with fresh earth, or otherwise caring for the birds.  The frame material is of 2 x 2-inch scantling at the corners, while the side strips are made of inch boards sawed 2 inches wide.  The earth under this run should be slightly mounded for the sake of dryness.

---

Whatever is worth doing at all is worth doing well.—Earl of Chesterfield.

## A PORTABLE CHICKEN COOP

One of the annoyances about an ordinary chicken coop is that it is not easily moved from place to place, nor provided with a yard. To obtain a yard the coop must be moved separately, and thus require the loss of more or less time. In the drawing shown herewith is a simple, homemade coop,

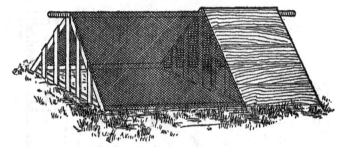

COOP EASILY MOVED

which can very easily be moved by the aid of the handles at the apex at each end. The coop is built of ordinary material on a base frame, and with a V-shaped roof and side frames. The ridge pole is extended, as shown at each end, to form a handle. A convenient length is about 2 feet for the coop and 3 or 4 feet for the yard. If desired, the hen may be allowed the freedom of the yard or may be held in by slats, as shown in the drawing.

## A HOMEMADE BROODER

The material costs about $2 and a handy person can build one in a day. The gas from the lamp does not go into the chick apartment at all, but filters around under the floor, making it dry and warm. The lamp flame is about 3 inches from the sheet iron. The heat flows up gently through the drum, *f*, which is perforated with holes in the side, thus letting part of the heat out into the hover and the balance in the brooder above. The heat reservoir, *g*, between the sheet iron, *k*, and the floor, *c*, is about 1 inch deep. The tube, *f*, should not touch the sheet iron, merely extending through the floor, *c*. It takes very little oil.

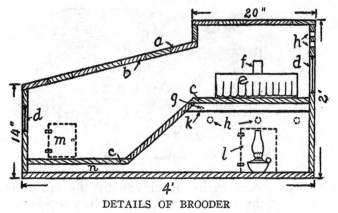

DETAILS OF BROODER

In the cut, *a*, is the paper roofing over inch-matched boards, *b*; *c* is board floor of same material; *d* are small windows, *e* is the hover, *h* are holes in each side of the brooder for the escape of gas and fumes, *l* shows door to reach the lamp, *n* air space below the floor.

## MOVABLE BROODER HOUSE

The type of house shown in the cut is one of the best for raising poultry. It may be built on runners, with a tight board floor of matched boards. A convenient size is 6 feet wide and 10 feet long, 6 feet high in front and 4 feet at the rear. The door is in the middle, and there is a window on each side, with two openings below. The roof should be covered with a good quality of prepared roofing.

HOUSE ON RUNNERS

The same material used to cover the sides will make the house warmer. Roosts may be put in after the brooders are taken out, and the chickens easily protected from foxes and other animals.

## A VERY CHEAP HENHOUSE

It was built by a "down east" Yankee. The studs and rafters were made of two pieces of 1 x 2-inch stuff nailed together T shape. These were set up 2 feet 10 inches apart on centers and covered with wire netting drawn taut. This was then covered with tarred paper, which made the only material between the fowls and the outside air. They have wintered in these houses without discomfort, and gave a good egg yield. The wire netting prevented the paper from sagging when the house was covered with snow.

They can who think they can.

## A DAYLIGHT CHICKEN CATCHER

Do you, when you want fried chicken on short notice, run it down, provided it doesn't run you down? Here is a better way. Fasten a barrel hoop securely to a handle about 6 feet long, and to it fasten a bag about 3 feet deep. A piece of an old hammock is fine for a bag, or horse net or fish net —anything the chicken cannot get out of. Lay it on the ground, call the chicken and throw the corn over the bag, and when one suitable goes on lift up the hoop and you have it. If the bag is made not over 1 foot deep it can be dropped down over the chicken while eating.

## A SIMPLE HAWK TRAP

Make a box 4 inches deep, 6 inches square and nail to a 4-foot pole with cleats at the bottom to keep from turning over. Cover top of box with 1-inch mesh wire. Place a little chicken in the box; then put a steel trap on top of box and set it out under the trees where the hawks lodge to watch for the chickens. If there are hawks around, it is pretty sure to catch them.

## SCARE AWAY CROWS AND HAWKS

For keeping hawks and crows away from the poultry yards, get a few bright tin shingles, link them together with wire, and hang upon an arm extending from the top of a high pole, where sun and wind strike fairly. The jingle and glitter is sufficient to keep these pests at a safe distance. You will also find them useful in the corn and melon fields where crows are troublesome.

## PRACTICAL HIVES AND HIVE MAKING

VERY apiarist knows that there is no item in bee keeping of more practical importance than the hive and brood frame. The Langstroth, or Simplicity size of frame has become almost standard, for there are more frames of this size in use than all others combined. The frame proper is 17⅝ inches long, 9⅛ inches deep, and the top bar is 19 inches long. There are several styles made, but many prefer what is known as the Hoffman. This has a heavy top bar in depth, as well as width. The ends, or end bars, are made 1⅜ inches wide for about 3 inches down and one side is worked off to a knife edge, which comes against the square edge of the next frame, making them self-spacing, but not a closed-end frame, and allowing the proper bee space between the top bars. This works fairly well without the use of the honey board, though one is preferable.

The hive for this frame, to be best adapted to the production of comb or extracted honey, should contain 10 frames, the inside dimensions being 15 inches wide, 10 inches deep and 18⅜ inches long. A follower can be used at one side to assist in removing frames by first removing the follower or division board. This arrangement leaves ⅜ inch between the top of the frames and the top of the brood nest, so that when the surplus cases are put on the proper bee space is

DOUBLE-WALLED HIVE

preserved. This hive is made of scant ½-inch lumber for the outside, ship-lapped together in a manner to make a perfect joint. It is 20 inches wide, 24 inches long, about 20 inches high to the eaves, or roof, outside measurements, and weighs complete about 50 pounds. The inside dimensions of the brood nest should be the same as any 8 or 10-frame hive, as the bee keeper may prefer. The brood nest is raised sufficiently to admit of packing between it and the hive proper, also a space for packing at ends and sides.

DOVETAILED HIVE

The lower portion of the hive being well protected against the cold, the warmth of the bees will care for the upper portion. To avoid condensation cover the brood nest after removing the surplus cases with a porous substance, or chaff cushion. Make a wooden rim about 4 inches deep, covering the top and bottom with burlap and filling with wheat chaff or cut straw. Many prefer the cut straw both for cushions and packing the hives. This rim should be made a little smaller than the inside of the hive.

In extremely warm weather the cover can be raised a few inches in front, giving a circulation of air all around the surplus department, and shading it at the same time. The cover is hinged at the back end, and when raised, as shown in cut, makes two shelves for the use of the operators, which are highly appreciated; besides, there is no lifting on or off of covers, as is the case in other hives. The alighting board is hinged and can touch the ground, which is of great advantage to the bees during a heavy flow of honey.

Perhaps there are more single-walled hives used in the United States than double-walled or chaff hives, but in northern states a double-walled hive is preferable.

## DEVICE FOR EXTRACTING BEESWAX

Wax, as produced by the bees and worked into comb, is almost pure white, but, on being melted

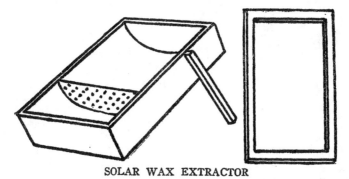

SOLAR WAX EXTRACTOR

and cooled, is yellow. A man who knows advises every beekeeper to use the solar wax extractor.

All that is necessary is to have a box with glass to fit over it, as shown in the drawing. To melt combs, put in the box an old dripping-pan, having a hole at one corner, and that corner the lowest, with some kind of a dish set under to catch the wax. Set in the sun. To get the most out, break up the combs into fine pieces, then soak in water for a day or two longer before rendering.

## SELF-FEEDER FOR BEES

A very simple device for feeding bees on syrup may be made if you take an ordinary fruit can, fill it full of syrup and over the top tie a thick rag with a string. Then invert the can in a small pan or dish. The syrup will seep out through the rag around the edges of the jar just fast enough for the bees to keep it cleaned up.

## GARDEN AND ORCHARD

### AN IRON HOOP TRELLIS

**T**HIS trellis is made of the iron hoops that are now used so commonly upon sugar and other barrels. They are of stout wire, welded into a complete circle, and, as barrels are constantly going to pieces, one can get together quite a collection of these, when they can be assorted into uniform sizes.

An attractive trellis is shown. Three strips of wood, pointed at the lower end and finished with a knob at the top, are provided, the length being a matter for individual taste. A trellis for tomato plants will need not more than two hoops, while one for sweet peas may require a half dozen. The strips of wood should be of inch board, 2 inches wide. The hoops are secured to the uprights by small staples made for putting up wire fencing. The wooden posts may be oiled or painted some attractive color. This trellis will be

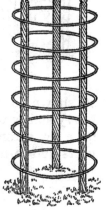

THE TRELLIS

greatly appreciated both in the vegetable and flower gardens, for its strength and attractiveness.

---

Diligence is the mother of good luck.—Franklin.

## PLANT SUPPORTS OF BARREL HOOPS

The ordinary wooden hoops from barrels may be made into an attractive trellis for grapes or a support for smaller twining plants by being arranged

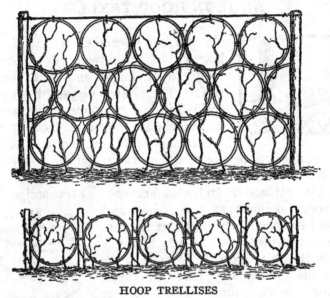

HOOP TRELLISES

as shown in the sketch. Attach them firmly to heavy stakes with some No. 7 smooth wire and you have an arrangement which will last for several years and is not unattractive to the eye.

## A FOLDING TRELLIS

A good way to pole beans is to make a folding trellis out of plastering lath, as shown in the cuts.

TRELLIS FOLDED

Bore three small holes through each lath, as shown in the first cut and fasten them together with common wire nails well clinched.

Five-foot posts are set 1 foot in the ground and a
wire strung at top and bottom. The lath are fastened
to the wires with string, as shown in the second
cut. The trellis is made in sections so as to be

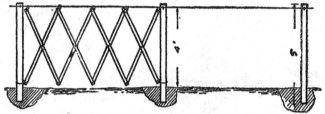

TRELLIS IN PLACE IN THE GARDEN

easily handled. When not in use it is folded up
and laid away under shelter. The posts are spaced
evenly so that one section of trellis will just go between two posts.

## EASY WAY TO POLE BEANS

Set posts at convenient distances apart and
stretch a wire at the top. This may be done as
soon as ground is plowed. Plant and cultivate one
row each side of line until beans begin to vine, then

TRELLIS FOR BEANS

set poles slanting, tying them together where they
cross at the wire. This braces the whole row and
beans can be cultivated with hoe. Hills 3 feet apart
in row with one vine to hill are better than two
vines.

## TRELLIS THAT STANDS ALONE

A plant support or garden trellis, such as shown in the drawing, is very handy in the garden. This

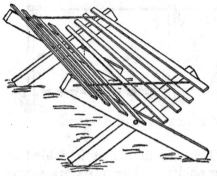

double form of trellis can be folded up and takes very little room in storage. All trellises and stakes should be gathered as soon as the crop is harvested and stored under cover until the next season. They are useful

DOUBLE FORM OF TRELLIS

for tomatoes, beans, peas, cucumbers and other plants that need some support. The double trellis is built of narrow ½-inch slats and pieces of 2 x 3, which are bolted together for the legs. The top may be held in place by pieces of string or wire attached at the points indicated in the drawing. The length, width and height of this trellis should depend upon the use to be made of it. A large one will be wanted for a large spreading plant and a small one for a small plant. It is important to have trellises just the right size to give proper support.

## PROTECTING NEWLY SET PLANTS

Plants newly transplanted always demand more or less protection from the blighting effects of too much sun and wind. It is best achieved by making a shelter such as is shown in the cut. Two 10-

foot poles and two 3-foot pieces of any convenient
thickness for the crosspieces, with four 14-inch
weather-strips for the legs, constitute the frame.
In the middle of it two hooks should be inserted on
each side, and upon these the covering fastened,
which can thus be adjusted very quickly.  The covering may consist of burlap or any kind of rough
sacking.

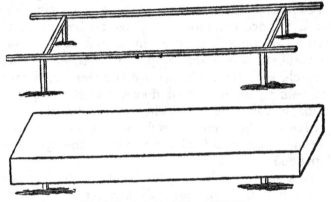

FRAME OPEN AND COVERED

Being so simple and economical to make, it is
advisable to have enough frames to protect the
number of tender plants that are set out in a garden at one time.  They possess other advantages
than sheltering the young things from the direct
rays of the sun.  They allow slow evaporation, and
so keep newly watered ground moist for hours,
whereas if exposed to the sun and wind it would
soon become dry and caked.  On windy days it is
only necessary to let the sacking down on the wind-
ward side of the shelter.  In case of frost the protection that they afford is of inestimable value.

Love thy neighbor, yet pull not down thy hedge.

## MAKING THE HOTBED

The value of every vegetable garden can be greatly increased and the time during which a supply of fresh vegetables may be secured for the table greatly lengthened by the use of the common manure hotbed and the cold frame. These indispensable adjuncts of the good garden are so easily made and cost so little that it is surprising they are not more common. A good hotbed made the latter part of February or in March can be made to yield an abundant supply of lettuce, radishes, spinach, etc., for table use by the time such crops are being planted out of doors, and the supply of cabbage, tomatoes and other plants for the home garden can be secured ready to transplant several weeks earlier than if plants grown in the open were depended upon.

As a source of heat fresh horse manure is used. About half manure and half fine straw mixed together should be piled in square piles 2 or 3 feet in depth, and 4 or 5 feet in width and long enough to contain the amount necessary for the beds desired. After heating has well started, the piles should be forked over, turning the outside of the old pile to the inside of the new, and when heating again is well under way the material is ready for use. In the meantime select a well-drained spot, sloping to the south, if possible.

Dig a trench 6½ feet wide, 2 feet deep and as long as desired, running east and west. Now place the manure in the trench, tramping and packing in thin, even layers until level with the surface. Make a frame 6 feet wide and as long as desired, but some multiple of three, because the hotbed sash are always made 3 feet wide. The end piece should be 9 inches high in front and 15 inches high in the back. The front side board should be 9 inches wide and for the rear it will require two boards, preferably 12 and 3, with the wide one at the top.

A frame 12 or 15 feet in length will be quite large enough for the ordinary farm garden. Set this frame on top of the manure with the slope facing the south and secured by stakes. On top of the manure put 6 inches of good garden soil and cover the frame with common sash or windows 6 feet long by 3 feet wide. At first the heat will run very high, but in a few days it will fall to 80 or 90 degrees, when it is safe to plant the seeds.

## MAKING PERMANENT HOTBEDS

Hotbed sash should be constructed of white pine or of cypress, and the sash bars should run in one direction only, and that lengthwise of the sash. The bars may be braced through the middle by a transverse bar placed through the long bars below the glass. The two ends of the sash should be made of sound timber, 3 inches wide at the top and 4 inches wide at the bottom end, mortised to receive the ends of the sash bars, and with a tenon at the ends to pass through the side pieces, which should be 2½ inches wide.

A permanent hotbed should be so constructed as to be heated either with fermenting manure or by radiating pipes from the dwelling or greenhouse heating plant. For a permanent bed, in which manure is to supply the heat, a pit 2 to 2½ feet deep, according to the latitude in which the work is to be done, should be provided.

The sides and ends may be supported by a lining of plank supported by posts 4 feet apart, or, what is better still, a brick wall 9 inches thick, as shown in the drawing, may be used.  In either case the pit lining should come flush with the surface of the soil.  The site for the pit should be on naturally well-drained land, and a tile drain from the bottom of the excavation should be provided to prevent the

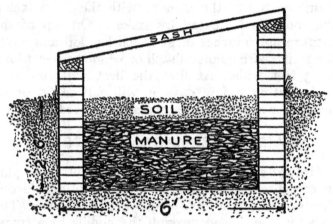

HOTBED WITH BRICK WALLS

water from accumulating in the pit and stopping the fermentation of the manure during the period the hotbed is in use.

Standard hotbed sash are 3 by 6 feet.  The pit, therefore, should be some multiple of 3 feet in length, and the width should be the same as the length of the sash, 6 feet.  The plank frame, or the brickwork of the pit, may be extended above the surface of the ground sufficiently to allow for placing the sash immediately upon these permanent structures.

## HEAT FOR HOTBEDS

Make an excavation 5 x 16 feet on the surface, and about a foot deep.  Lengthwise along this

space lay three rows of tiling, one along the center
and one about a foot from each side. The tiles
should be 4 inches inside measure, and 1 foot long.
These are placed end to end so as to fit closely,
and earth is pressed around them so as to hold
every piece exactly in place. Then the excavation
is filled with rich soil until level with the surface,
excepting at the end the tiles are left bare for
a few inches. The board frame, 5 x 15 feet, is
next put in place so as to leave 6 inches of each
row of tiles projecting beyond the ends of the
frame.

At the east ends of the bed, a hole should be dug
3 x 4 feet on surface and 2 feet deep; in this hole
a crude fireplace may be made of loose brick and
the flue connected with the three ends of projecting
tile. At the west end of the frame a brick chamber should be made into which the three tiles
enter, giving them a common flue for outlet.
Cover the top of this chamber closely, excepting a
6-inch circular hole, into which a single length of
stovepipe is fitted. A sloping door is hung over the
fireplace cavity to keep out the rain; and the earth
raised high enough around to prevent surface water
from running into the hole. Bank soil about the
frame. You may happen to have on hand six old
storm window sashes of that size. Of course the
sashes slope to the south in the usual way.

When the fire is kindled in the fireplace the
smoke comes freely from the stovepipe. The tiles
are covered with soil to a depth of about 6 inches.
With a good fire, you can quickly warm up the
earth on the coldest days of spring. And when
once well heated, the earth and tiling hold the heat
for a long time, provided the draft is closed. Unlike
beds heated with manure, the heat supply can thus

be regulated to suit the demand of the prevailing weather.

## COLD FRAMES AND THEIR MANAGEMENT

In the South cold frames are in use all winter. The principal winter crops grown are lettuce, radishes, beets, cauliflower and occasionally cabbage, while these crops are commonly followed in spring by cucumbers, cantaloups and sometimes Irish potatoes. The frames are easily made. Rough inch lumber (heart pine is best in the South, and hemlock in the North) and 2 x 4 or 2 x 3-inch scantling are all that is required. For the double frames, strips 3 inches wide and ¾ or ½ inch thick, long enough to extend across the frame, should be provided for rafters. The back or north side of the single frame should be 12 or 15 inches high, while the front should slope down to 8 inches. In Southern practice, where canvas covers are used, the back should be 2½ feet and all cracks should be well covered with building paper, held in place by laths tacked over it.

Good treatment for the posts used in construction is to dip them in kerosene over night. This will preserve them indefinitely. Drive the posts into the ground 18 inches and let them extend upward to the top of the boards, putting a post at the union of each pair of boards and nailing them to it. All ends and rafters may be made so that they can be quickly removed, so that the frames can be plowed and the ground prepared with a mule. The sides of the double frames are best made 1 foot high, with the ends sloping upward to 2½ feet. Down the center of the frame, a row of 2 x 4-inch posts 2½ feet above ground are set 8 feet apart.

Over each one of these a rafter is bent and fastened to the sides of the frames.

For cold frames in the North, glass is the only covering to be thought of. By all means, put the frames up facing the south or southeast and to afford protection against the north and northwest winds, cold the country over, a high wall, a thick hedge, or a piece of thick woodland should be close at the back of them.

The soil in the frames should be thoroughly prepared, rich and pulverized thoroughly. An abundance of well-rotted stable manure should be used; if thoroughly decomposed, at the rate of 75 to 100 tons an acre is not excessive, unless the soil is already very rich. Whether glass or canvas is used as a covering great attention must be given to water and ventilation. The land should be well drained that no water will stand, or the soil become water logged; that is one side of the water question, but in addition, the plants should be carefully watered from time to time to provide sufficient for their needs.

If the coverings are kept down too constantly, the growth of the plants will be weak and spindling and such diseases as damping off, Botrytis and drop will work havoc with them. Careful attention to watering, ventilation and keeping the surface of the ground stirred are the genuine secrets of controlling these pests. Watch the temperature, do not let it rise too high, lower it by raising the sash or drawing back the covers. The canvas covers should be drawn back a portion of every day when the temperature is not too low, and at other times the ends may be raised, to allow the air to circulate under them. A sharp eye must be kept on the frost item. Sometimes steam heat is provided, oil stoves may be used and glass covered frames should be covered with burlap or straw mats, securely held down either by tying them in place or by weighting them down. Both canvas and the glass covering should be well fastened to prevent their being lifted off by strong winds.

The upper end of glass sash may be held down with a hook and staple, a hook being placed on the back of the frame at the center of each sash with the staple in the end of the sash. Canvas covers are best held down by nailing along the center to a board run lengthwise on the center of the rafters, in the case of double coverings, or along the back in the case of single ones and by placing marbles or small pebbles in the cloth and tying about these every 4 or 5 feet, along the ends and sides, slipping the looped ends of the twine used in tying them over nails driven into the ends and sides of the frame.

## A HAND GARDEN CULTIVATOR

Now that garden crops are planted almost exclusively in rows a tool that will clean out the weeds, stir the soil around the plants, and, by making a good surface mulch, prevent the loss of moisture to some extent, is essential for the proper care of the garden. The wheel hoe of our cultivator is usually used for this purpose by the professional gardener, but the price is generally considered rather high by the ordinary farmer or amateur.

This machine, although homemade and not very handsome in appearance, does the work as well as a $6 or $8 tool, and cost not more than 40 cents to make. For a wheel, take the fly wheel of an old sewing machine, about 1 foot in diameter, and put a round bolt tightly through the axle. Then a piece of plank, *a*, 20 x 10 inches, and cut as shown, boring holes for the axle where marked. After the wheel is set in place, it should turn easily and steadily, if balanced properly. For the handle, *c c*, cut out and round from a piece of plank two pieces, or use any that may be otherwise obtained. Then get a blacksmith to make three teeth, *b*, out of a

HAND CULTIVATOR

piece of spring steel 1 inch wide and 8 inches long, bent as shown. Two-inch holes are drilled through them for screws.

One tooth should be placed about 6 inches behind the wheel and directly in the center, the other two being 4 inches behind the first, and the same distance from the center tooth. When this cultivator is pushed through the rows it should run with little pressure from the operator, clearing out the weeds and stirring the soil at the same time. This contrivance does the work well, and if given two coats of brown and green paint it will be improved in appearance.

---

Know thy opportunity.—Pittacus.

## A CONVENIENT GARDEN STOOL

This device will prove useful in doing hand work in the garden. It is made from two barrel staves  upon which is mounted a low stool. This should be narrow, so that it may be drawn between the rows of vegetables. The holes in the seat

WEEDING STOOL are large enough for the fingers to go through and render the stool more easily handled. The device is especially convenient for the women.

## WATERING SEED SOIL MADE EASY

To avoid disturbing small seeds by watering, when planted in forcing boxes, a plan has been devised which not only insures against the disturbance of the seed, but keeps the soil of the entire box in a moderate state of moisture, which is an essential feature in early growth.

Make a box of any desired size to suit the occasion, and about 3 inches deep. Then get a few small unglazed flower pots and place same on stove until quite hot. With a short piece of candle, seal drain hole in bottom of pots, taking care not to put wax over the entire bottom of pot. Place pots in box about 9 inches apart on a thin layer of sand, and overlap pieces of broken pots, to convey by capillary attraction the water to the entire soil of the box, which soil should be sifted and box filled to within ¼ inch of the top of the pots.

Cover the box with glass, and heat from above will draw the water up to the roots. By this method you will not have surface baking, which is so troublesome with surface watering. If so desired, you can cover the pots with circular pieces of pasteboard or tin, and avoid surface evaporation from the pots. Always fill pots with warm water.

## CATCHING OWLS AND HAWKS

A friend of ours captured a large owl and fastened him securely with a small chain to a stake in the middle of an open field. He set three posts 5 feet tall and 4 to 5 inches in diameter 20 to 30 yards from the owl, and on each post placed a small steel trap with a bunch of hay or grass tied to the post just under the trap, to hide it, as shown in cut. At night, the owl called. Others came, and seeing nothing near, alighted in the trap on the post. During the day hawks came, and were caught in the same way. In two months two owls and 17 hawks were caught. In some places a bounty is paid, so there is a profit in two ways. The owl may be fed on the hawks caught and on rabbits or chickens that may die around the premises.

TRAP ON POST

The most difficult part of this scheme is often the capture of the first owl, but if you are a good hunter you will find a way.

---

Make no absolute promises, for nobody will help you to perform them.

Money is a good servant, but a bad master.

## MOVING A LARGE TREE

To move a large tree one may find it very satisfactory to use a rig similar to that shown in the
picture.  Make a three-sided standard of 2 x 4-inch
stuff.  Loosen the dirt around the roots of the tree

RIG FOR MOVING TREE

and wrap the tree firmly at the base with old
carpet or burlap to prevent injury.  Place the
standard firmly in the ground and tie the crosspiece to the body of the tree with strong rope to
each side of the standard and hitch a horse to the

other end.  With a slow pull the tree can be drawn onto the drag and then hauled to the new location. It can be placed in the ground again by using the standard in the same way it was used to load it upon the drag.

———————

A penny saved is two pence clear,
A pin a day's a groat a year.—Benjamin Franklin.

The man who builds, and wants wherewith to pay,
Provides a home from which to run away.—Young.

———————

## TRANSPLANTING TREES

Here is a way to transplant large trees that is not so difficult as such transplanting is by many supposed to be.  The first move to make is to dig all round the tree, leaving a large ball of soil, which is carefully wrapped in sacking or canvas to hold it on the roots and prevent drying. When this is well tied in place a chain is passed round the ball two or three times and hooked, as shown in Figure 1.
Then with a pair

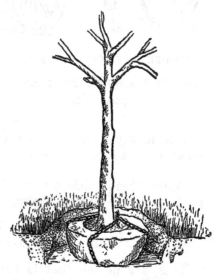

FIGURE I—BALLED

of heavy wheels on a short axle and a strong pole laid across it, with a massive iron hook fastened to the pole, it is easy to back up to the tree. The sketch, Figure 2, shows the truck with its lever raised ready to hook into the chain. The rope at the end of the pole brings it down and the tree up, when the pole is fastened under a second pair of wheels. The young trunk must be kept from contact with the machinery by the free use of blankets and bags. The secret of success in transplanting trees is to injure the roots as little as possible.

FIGURE 2—HOOK AND TRUCK

The manly part is to do with might and main what you can do.—Emerson.

Many things difficult to design prove easy to performance.—Samuel Johnson.

## HOMEMADE FRUIT PICKER

This is a device that is hard to beat for reaching fruit at the top of tall trees. After a little practice, a man can operate it rapidly, far out-stripping hand pickers and at the same time not

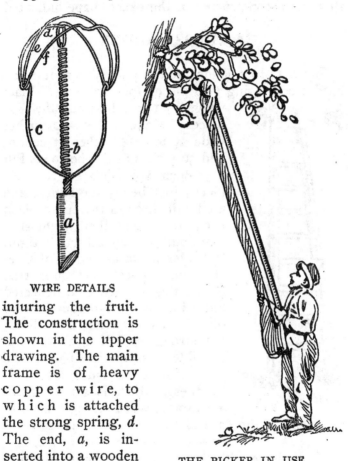

WIRE DETAILS

THE PICKER IN USE

injuring the fruit. The construction is shown in the upper drawing. The main frame is of heavy c o p p e r w i r e, to w h i c h is attached the strong spring, *d*. The end, *a*, is inserted into a wooden handle as long as needed. When the muslin sack is attached, as shown in the picture of the picker in use, the jaws of the picker are easily closed by pulling slightly on the cloth. The fruit falls through the sack or long cloth tube into the hand of the operator. Many devices have been made for this sort of service, but it will be hard to find one that works better than this one if constructed in the exact shape indicated.

## A TRUSS LADDER

For a 14-foot ladder select four pieces of 1 x 2 hard wood, using two pieces for each side.   Place

rungs of 1 x 2 between the side pieces.  Make ladder 12 inches wide at top, 14 inches at center, and 30 inches at the bottom. Put a ¼-inch bolt through the side pieces just below the rungs, and a 6d nail through the end of each rung to prevent them from slipping out.   Keep all bolts tight. A ladder made as above, of Oregon pine, 14 feet long, supported on trestles at each end, deflected but 1 inch when 150 pounds were placed on the center.  It is light, yet strong, and it is almost impossible to spring it.  The special advantage of a truss ladder is lightness, which is a very great

THE LADDER     advantage, when strength is combined, as in the case of this particular ladder.

---

Let us have faith that right makes might; and in that faith let us to the end do our duty as we understand it.—Lincoln.

Never spend your money before you've earned it.  Never buy what you do not want; it is not cheap.

## ORCHARD LADDER ON WHEELS

The accompanying sketch shows the manner of construction. Any farmer or orchardist can build it. Secure two old mower wheels and one piece of 2 x 4 scantling for an axle. Place the ladder upon this scantling. To keep it upright use poles, two at the bottom and one near the top of the ladder, extending to the ground. The upper one should be forked at the top so as to hold the ladder firmly. This ladder is 18 feet high, and

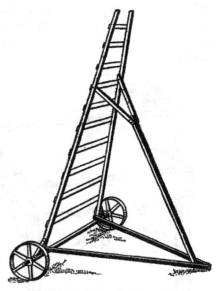

LADDER FOR FRUIT TREES

as the foundation is broad, there is no danger of it falling over. The brace is so made that it can be adjusted, thus enabling one to place the ladder at any angle.

## CONVENIENT SORTING TABLES

Where fruit is packed from the trees a sorting table will always be found convenient. It generally saves time and labor to do the packing right in the orchard. A handy table is one mounted on wheels which may be of any size desired and should be large enough to hold at least four barrels. The

wheels can be picked up from discarded machinery
or quickly made by nailing together crosswise two
boards to prevent them from splitting, boring a
hole in the center for the axle and rounding them
off with a key hole saw.  One end of the table
should be made several inches higher than the
other, so that the culls will roll into a pile at the
lower end.

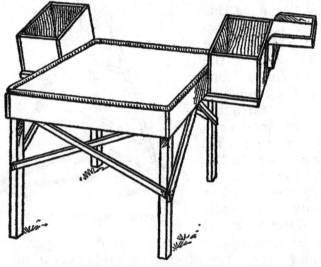

OREGON SORTING TABLE

In the Hood river district of Oregon a table such
as shown here is commonly used.  This is made to
accommodate two packers.  To make such a table
take four standards about 3 feet high.  It is made
3 x 4 feet in size, the top covered with strong burlap or canvas and allowed to hang rather loosely.
Saw off the tops of the legs on a bevel so as not to
have the sharp corners push into the burlap, and
make points that will bruise or cut the fruit.

A piece of old garden hose is generally nailed around the top of the table to protect the fruit. Besides the braces shown in the cut it is also well to wire the legs and braces together firmly, as there is a heavy load to support. The shelves on each side are for holding the boxes, as all the good fruit in this region is boxed. The height is only relative, the point being to construct it so each packer can work with the greatest comfort, avoiding back bending in all cases. The top should not be greater than 3 x 4 feet, as anything larger would not allow two packers to reach all points of it without unnecessary stretching.

## PORTABLE HAY DERRICK

 VERY satisfactory derrick for stacking hay is shown in the sketch. The base pieces are 6 x 6 inches by 16 feet. For the center pole we use a straight round pole 7 inches in diameter at the base and 5 inches at the top about 24 feet long. We put an iron band around the base and insert the peg upon which it turns. About halfway to the top is an iron collar, which has three loops to it that form an attachment for the braces, which are fastened about 15 feet from the bottom of the central pole. This allows the pole to turn readily when in upright position. The top framework is made of 2 x 6-inch pieces

HAY DERRICK

12 feet long. The rigging, consisting of three pulleys and the hay rope, is attached as shown in sketch. By having the lower pole attached near the base of the upright the arms will make half a turn when the hay fork is lifted, thus swinging around from the ground or wagon onto the stack.

## A WIRE TIGHTENER

Here is a device easily made and very convenient to use in tightening barbed wire when stringing it upon the posts. Cut out a piece of inch board in the shape shown in the picture with a notch to let in the face of a hammer. Insert a long bolt at the point indicated by the light dotted lines, to prevent splitting. Fasten on the hammer with leather straps. The

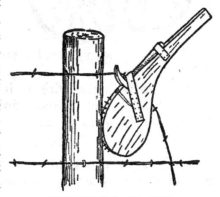

TIGHTENER IN USE

sharp brads should stick out about half an inch. Carefully finish the handle so that it will be smooth and not hurt the hands when you are using the device. It should be made of tough hardwood.

## FENCE WIRE REEL

Here is a device on which one can wind barbed wire that is much better than an old barrel. The reel is mounted on a truck made of old buggy wheels with short shafts. The cart may be drawn along by a man while a boy steadies the reel to keep it from unwinding too rapidly. For winding up wire, the machine is best pushed just fast enough

WIRE REEL ON WHEELS

to keep up with the wire as it is being wound on the reel. A crank placed upon the reel proves serviceable in winding up.

Never sign a writing till you have read it; neither drink water till you have seen it.

One part of knowledge consists in being ignorant of such things as are not worthy to be known.

Get the work habit.

## SAFE WAY TO STRING BARBED WIRE

One of the most satisfactory ways to unreel barbed wire is to make a contrivance similar to the one shown on page 157. Fasten a short piece of plank to the front end of a stone boat. Bore a 2-inch hole in this plank and set the spool of barbed wire on top. Run a piece of gas pipe about 5 feet long through the spool and let the bottom end rest in the hole made in the plank.

Attach the stone boat to the rear end of the wagon and have an assistant sit in the wagon and hold the top end of the pipe. If the wire becomes kinked the assistant simply lets go of the pipe and the spool rolls off the boat without breaking the wire.

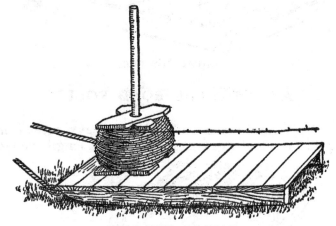

WIRE REEL ON BOAT

## A BOXED STONE BOAT

A flat stone boat or drag is convenient for many purposes, but its uses are limited because it has no great capacity. On page 158 is shown an arrangement for increasing the utility of a stone boat 100 per cent. It is made of plank and has sides 1 foot high. It may be used for the purpose for which the ordinary drag is employed, and in addition is very convenient for hauling apples, potatoes, or other root crops from the field.

By increasing the size of the box, manure can be

hauled out from stables as it is dumped into it from wheelbarrows without having to reload or wheel up an incline. It is low on the ground and very convenient for loading. All light, bulky articles, as well as heavy stones, bags of fertilizers and seed, can easily be hauled on this contrivance.

CAPACIOUS DRAG

## A HOMEMADE ROAD ROLLER

If you need a road roller get a heavy sheet iron cylinder, stand it on end and place a length of 1½

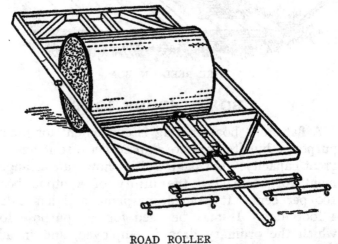

ROAD ROLLER

or 2-inch pipe through the center. The end should be placed on planks which are well soaked or are well oiled, and the pipe braced to keep it exactly in the center. Fill the cylinder with good concrete, and when it has set tip it over and build a frame for it, so you can hitch a removable tongue at either side. The frame should be made of good strong hardwood well braced. The cuts show plainly just how the roller is made and put together.

## AN OLD-FASHIONED DROGUE

Drogue is an old-fashioned word applied to a low drag or sled, something like the stone boat in general use now. The word is seldom heard today.

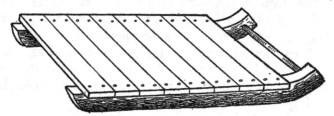

HOMEMADE HANDY DROGUE

So accustomed are we to the regulation stone boat that most of us do not know that there is still a more handy arrangement that is fully as easy to build and better to use, because it cannot slide sidewise on a hill. Select a small tree that has a bend in it the shape of a sled runner and split it with a sharp saw while it is green. It saws fastest and easiest while frozen. Saw or hew the bottom and top flat, so planks about 4 feet long may be pinned to it. Bore the front ends so a heavy stake with a shoulder may be inserted to prevent the runners from drawing together, and the drogue is done. It is handy for all work, but may need side rails spiked to it, if small stones are to be drawn.

Regular boat planks are not easy to obtain now that the old up and down saws are not in use.

## A DITCHING SCRAPER

There should be a ditching scraper on every farm. They can be purchased made of steel, but a homemade one costs little and is quite service-able. Take two planks, each 10 inches wide and 3 feet long, of good 2-inch hardwood. Bolt to them securely a pair of old plow handles. To the bottom bolt an old crosscut saw blade which will make a sharp edge. Let this project about an inch at the bottom. Attach two singletree hooks near each end of the lower board and your scraper is ready to use. With this scraper and two men a ditch can be cut one-quarter mile long and as deep as it could be plowed with a turning plow in two days' time. It is also very useful in filling holes in the highway.

## BRIDGE FOR A SMALL STREAM

For crossing a small creek or deep ditch a cheap bridge can be built as shown in the illustration. The lumber used is 6 inches wide and 2 inches thick, except for the floor and four side braces.

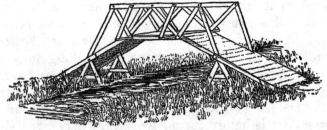

A BRIDGE OF TRIANGLES

Saw 11 pieces the length required for each of the two sides, then bore bolt holes 1½ inches from each end. Use ⅝-inch bolts 8½ inches long where four pieces come together and 6½-inch bolts where

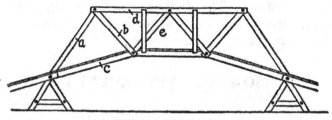

FRAMEWORK OF BRIDGE

three pieces meet. The A-shaped supports and the pieces for the approaches are bolted on at once, and then the side braces are put on. The sides of the bridge are made entirely of triangles. The first triangle is made of pieces, *a*, *b* and *c*. The second triangle of the pieces, *b*, *d* and *e*. The piers may be posts, stone or concrete.

## DAM FOR FARM POND

A small pond held by a good-sized hydraulic dam supplies water for house, barn and two acres

EASILY BUILT DAM

of garden and fruit, also floods a cranberry meadow
when needed. A section of the dam is placed 6
feet apart and covered with plank fitted tight. The
apron is of 12-foot plank spiked to the sills so as to
break joints. The bottom is made tight with
brush and clay. Stones are piled in behind the
plank coverings, as shown in cut.

## SOWING SEED EVENLY

These drawings show the construction of a wheel
seeding device that can be easily made at home.

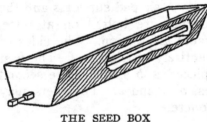

The axle is tightly
fitted into the
wheels so that it
turns when the
wheels do. This
agitates the grain
or other seed and
helps to keep the

THE SEED BOX

seed running out of the holes at the lower back
side of the box. The quantity of flow may be
regulated at pleasure by making the holes large
or small and increasing or diminishing the number
of holes.

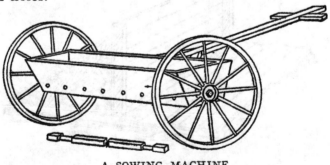

A SOWING MACHINE

It may be found desirable to have a considerable number of holes and then having plugs, for alternate ones, perhaps, which may be removed to make the seeding thicker. From 4 to 6 feet is suggested for the length of the box. Any old wheels will do if they are not too heavy to be easily drawn by hand.

## BERRY CRATE CARRIER

One of the most convenient appliances for use in the strawberry field is illustrated in the picture shown herewith. It shows a novel use for the old-fashioned yoke used so commonly on the old-time farms. The picture is so readily understood that no description need be given. This also suggests the many purposes for which a yoke may be used on a farm. Every farmer ought to have one, to make more easy the task of carrying things. In

YOKE CRATE CARRIER

some places yokes may be found for sale, but if you cannot buy one, make one yourself. Take a piece of strong, tough wood, shape it out to fit around the neck and shoulders and taper off the ends to what you consider the right size. Usually a groove is cut around about 1½ inches from each end and

a rope is securely tied. At the other end of the rope
a hook is attached the right size to go around the
bail handle of any ordinary pail. The hook may
be iron or may be formed from a strong, branched
stick.

## HANDY LOADING DEVICE

Here is a rig simple and strong that works well
for loading corn in the field. The picture shows

LOADING RIG IN USE

the construction of the rack and hoisting device
with pulley attachment. Such a rig will be found
useful for loading many things on a farm.

## RACK FOR HAULING FODDER

A handy rack for hauling fodder from the field
is shown in the drawing. It may be used for any
kind of corn, of course, for sorghum, and may be
found useful in moving brush. Each end of the

rack is hung from the axles by two straps of iron that can be obtained from any blacksmith at very little expense.

FODDER RACK

## PULLING FENCE POSTS

An easy and practical method of pulling fence posts, by which all digging and hand labor is eliminated, is here shown. Take a plank 4 feet long,

POST PULLER IN POSITION

1 foot wide and make a V-shaped notch in one end, nailing on several crosspieces to prevent splitting. This plank is used to change the horizontal draft to the vertical.

Place one end of chain around the post close to ground. Incline the plank against the post so the lower end of the plank will be about 1½ or 2 feet from the base of the post. Place the chain in the notch of the plank, start the team and the post in a few seconds will be clear of the ground.

In moving fences the chain should be attached to the rear axle of the wagon, so the posts may at once be loaded and hauled to the new location of the fence.

## ONE WAY TO PULL STUMPS

A Connecticut man has a very handy device for pulling peach stumps from old orchards, and can

TACKLE FOR STUMP-PULLING

pull 200 or more a day by this means. The limbs are cut off and the stumps, E, left as long as possible. A short rope or chain with a single pulley is attached to the top of the stump. The anchor rope, B, which runs through the pulley, is fastened to the bottom of a stout stump, A.

A pair of steady horses is attached to the rope and always pull toward the anchor stump. With a steady pull there is no jumping or jerking, and they will walk right off as if pulling a loaded wagon. Use about 60 feet of 1-inch rope, which costs $2.40, and the pulley, $1.75, making a total cost of $4.15.

## SIMPLE LAND MEASURE

Having much land measuring to do that requires greater accuracy than just " stepping it off," make a simple affair like this. The manner of construction is made plain. Use hardwood pieces; ⅝ or ¾ x 1 inch is heavy enough. Have lower points exactly 5 feet 6 inches apart. Make a round head on the handle. Grasp the top lightly in hand, holding at the side, whirl handle to bring rear point to front, moving off in direction to be measured. Continue to revolve measure, changing points in advancing. It takes three lengths to the rod.

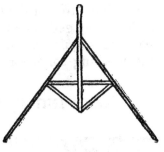

THE MEASURE

## STORING WATER

An easy way to make a reservoir at the spring is to throw up a bank, perhaps laying a wall first, founding it below the surface. Should the soil be such that water percolates through it, face the soil with loam on top and puddle it well. If this leaks, face it with clay and puddle the clay. These rules apply to all dams made of stone and earth.

Pipes entering reservoirs should enter at the bottom and the soil be well puddled around them to prevent the water working through beside the pipe. Each pipe must have a strainer over its supply end and have no air holes in its entire length.

A good strainer can be made from a piece of large lead pipe punched full of holes. One end may be flattened or turned over and the other drawn on over the end of the water pipe. Let nobody suppose that simple, inexpensive arrangements are faulty because primitive. If constructed correctly and in line with natural laws, they are not only all right, but are preferable to fancy, complicated devices that get out of order easily or in a year or two and require a master mechanic to put them into working condition again.

## GETTING A SUPPLY OF FUEL

 A PLAN for getting up the year's supply of fuel is suggested as follows: Fell the trees on the ground with a small sapling under them, so a log chain can be passed beneath. Then a logging bob (Figure 1) is tipped up on its side near the end of the log; a chain is hooked to the bolster near the ground, passed under the log and over the top runner of the bob and the team hitched to the end of the chain. A quick pull of the team and the bob comes down on both runners, with the log on the top of the bolster.

The log is now drawn to some sheltered place near the woodhouse and sawed into stove lengths with a 6-inch crosscut saw on the skidway shown in Figure 2. The limbs are trimmed in the woods, drawn on a pair of bobs to the shop, where there is a three-horse power boiler and two-horse power engine, and are sawed at the rate of 1½ cords an

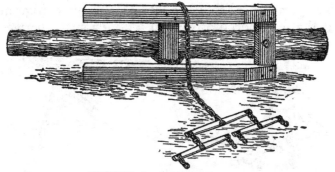

FIGURE I—LOGGING BOB

hour with a buzz saw. A handy device can be made of two crotched limbs, as shown in Figure 3, to saw large limbs on. A 2-inch auger hole is

FIGURE 2—SKIDWAY

bored where the limbs branch, and a hardwood limb driven tightly into the hole.

The following described device (Figure 4) is very handy to hold and lower the tree after sawing the stump off. [*a*, planks with holes bored in them; *b*, log; *c*, chain; *d*, crotched limb; *ee*, lever; *f*, iron pins.] It is made of two hardwood planks about 8 x 5 inches and 1½ inches thick bolted together at the top and bottom, with a 2-inch space between

FIGURE 3—HANDY SAWHORSE

for the lever to work in. One-inch holes are bored through the sides of both planks, in which iron pins are placed for the lever to pry over. The lever is made of white ash, and has two notches near the large end, with a chain link attached midway be-

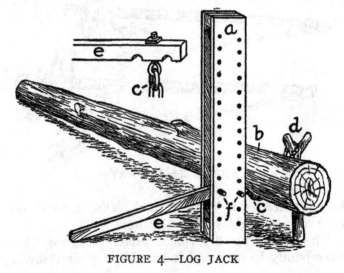

FIGURE 4—LOG JACK

tween notches. A stout chain is hooked in the link, passed under the log, and attached to a crotched limb leaning slightly against the opposite side of the log. By working the small end of the lever up and down and moving the pins up one hole at a time, a good-sized tree can be raised from the ground high enough to be sawed easily without a backache.

## SIMPLEST OF ALL CAMPING TENTS

The great trouble with camping-out tents is the weight of the frame, but the weight of the latter in

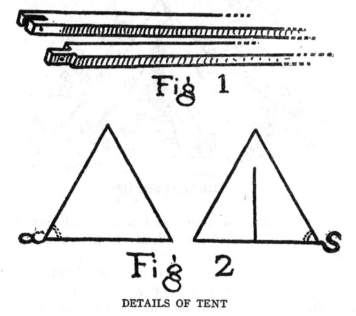

DETAILS OF TENT

the case of the tent figured herewith will hardly prove a burden to anyone, as only two light sticks are used, such as are shown in Figure 1. These are pressed into the ground 8 or 10 feet apart, according to the size of the tent, and brought together and fastened at the upper ends with such a joint as is shown, or with a string passing through a screw-eye in each pole, if a simpler method is preferred.

The tent is made from four triangular pieces of cloth, as suggested in Figure 2. One of these is cut up the center and hemmed, to afford an entrance to the tent. The triangular pieces are sewed together at the edges and at two of the opposite

THE TENT SET UP

corners pieces of stout cord are sewed into the corners of the cloth, the cloth being reinforced as suggested in the cut.

Two stout pegs of wood and two lighter ones are provided. To pitch the tent, put up the two frame poles A-fashion and draw the tent cloth over them, opposite seams and corners fitting over the poles. Draw out the other two corners and tie by the ropes to the stout pegs which have been driven into the ground. The two lighter pegs are used to fasten back the flaps of the front. It may be found well to hem a light cord into the bottom of the side having the opening, leaving the flaps free from the cord. The position of the cord is shown by the dotted line. It will not be in the way when lying across the opening of the tent on the ground and will strengthen the whole when the outer corners are drawn tightly up to the stout pegs.

This makes a practically square tent and the size can be as large or small as may be desired. To cut the side pieces, decide on the width of the sides and the height you wish the tent to be. Then draw a triangle (Figure 2), having the base as long as desired for the side of the tent, and a perpendicular 2 feet longer than the height desired for the tent, since the four sides of the tent are to be inclined, and must, therefore, be enough longer to make up for this.

This will prove a very satisfactory tent for boys who are camping out, and it has the merit of being easily made and very easy to carry about.

## GATES AND DOORS

## KEEPING A GATE FROM SAGGING

THE average farm gate is heavy, and after a little time it sags. When they get this way it takes a strong man to open and shut one. Here is a remedy. Get a wheel, either big or little, from an old piece of machinery, and bolt it to the front end of the gate in such a way that the gate will be held level. Now the smallest child can open

OLD PLOW WHEEL DOES THE TRICK

the gate for you. Try it, for it is a saver—saves your patience, your back and the gate.

174

## AN EASILY OPENED GATE

Take an old buggy wheel and fasten it as shown in the drawing to the gates that are opened often. The piece of board indicated by *c* drops between

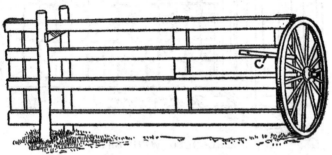

GOOD USE FOR A WHEEL

the spokes of the wheel and holds the gate either open or closed. A child can easily operate the heaviest gate with this attachment.

## A GATE THAT NEVER SAGS

A farmer has used this gate for many years and never spent five minutes repairing it. Countersink two pieces and pin them together. Then set up two 2 x 4 pieces 2 feet higher than the gate so it can be raised in winter. Mortise and set in between the cross-

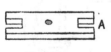

CROSSPIECE

pieces, which are 12 inches apart, the board, *a*, and fasten a cap to the top of the frame. The gate is 16 feet long, 12 feet being for the gateway and 4 feet for the weights to balance it. The frame is of 2 x 4s. Cover the 4-foot end with boards and fill with enough stones to balance it when hung.

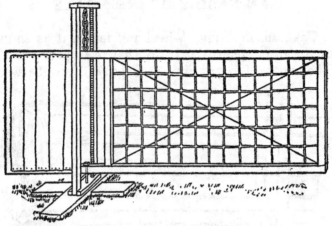

BALANCED WIRE GATE

Cover the gate with wire fencing and hang by a chain. Put a bolt through the lower part of the frame into the crosspiece, *a*.

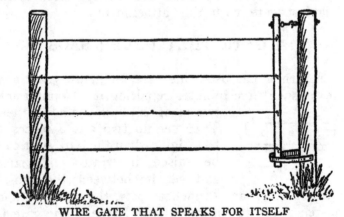

WIRE GATE THAT SPEAKS FOR ITSELF

## A CHEAP GATE

A light, useful and durable gate can be made of sassafras poles and barbed wire, as shown in the cut. Set a strong post 4 feet in the ground in the middle of the gateway and balance the gate on it.

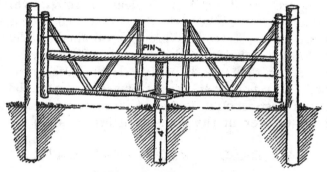

POLE AND WIRE GATE

The lower rail is made of two forked sassafras poles securely nailed together so as to work around the post.

## A SIMPLE FARM GATE

Many like such a gate as that shown in the cut. Material to be used depends largely on the purpose for which the gate is made. For a paddock or pasture gate, make it out of seasoned boards 1 x 6 inches, 12 or 14 feet long. The posts supporting

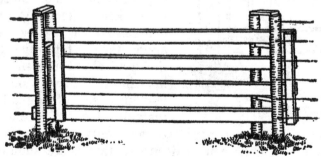

GATE SIMPLE AND STRONG

the gate are about 5 inches apart, the one on the inside being about 8 inches ahead of the other. They are joined together by cleats or rollers which support the gate and allow it to be pushed back and swing open. If rollers are not obtainable, cleats made of any hard wood are good. They need not be heavier than 1 x 4 inches. If the gate is to be used for a hog pasture, the lower cleats on both sets of posts should be placed just above the lower board to prevent the hogs from lifting it up.

## AN EASILY REGULATED GATE

The gate hanger illustrated in the drawing is very handy for use where it is desired to let hogs

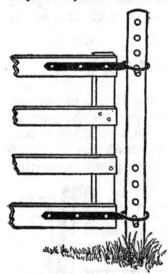

pass from one pasture to another while cows are confined to one. As shown, the hanger is a piece of strap iron bent around the post and supported by pegs. These pegs may be inserted in holes at varying heights. Raise the gate to let the hogs through and lower it to keep them in, of course. This is also a good device for raising the gate above the snow in winter. Many would find this use of the adjustable hanger prefer-

ADJUSTABLE HANGER

able to the gates made to raise only one end for snow. Of course it is desirable that there should be the least play as possible while the hanger slides up and down freely, and special care should be taken to set the post firmly. Otherwise the gate would sag.

## GATE TO OVERCOME SNOWDRIFTS

In the picture is shown a gate which can be readily adjusted to swing over snowdrifts. It is easily made from ordinary lumber. A 1 x 6-inch upright is used for the lower boards, 1 x 4 for the upper ones. The uprights at the hinge post are double 1 x 4, one piece outside and the other inside

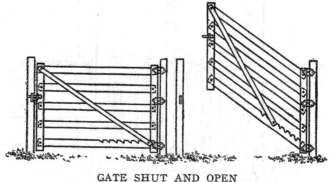

GATE SHUT AND OPEN

the bars. The upright at the latch side may be the same weight of stuff or slightly lighter, and fastened in the same way. Instead of nailing the bars to these uprights, bolts are used, one for each bar at each end. The lowest board is notched as shown, and the double brace used from the top of the latch post to the bottom of the hinge post. For the brace, 1 x 3 stuff is strong enough. They are joined near the bottom with a bolt, which engages with the notches when the gate is raised, as shown at the right.

## A TIME SAVER

To open and close gates that stock may be kept within bounds the year round is one thing which uses up a great deal of time, and makes no return. Every gate should be so made that it will fall into

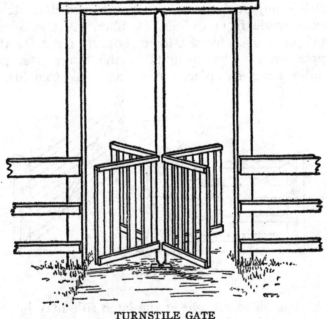

TURNSTILE GATE

place of its own weight and stay closed and open without hitch or bother. The cut illustrates a convenient thing that should be in larger use on farms. It is always open and always closed against stock. Put up and well painted, it will last for many years.

---

He who keeps company with great men is the last at the table and the first at any toil or danger.

## KEEP THE GATE OPEN

A simple and handy device which serves to hold the gate open is shown in the cut. To make it, procure a board, *a*, 1 x 4 x 12 inches and saw out a portion in the center, leaving a space on each side ½ inch wide, and bore holes for a bolt. Next get an 8-inch stick, *b*, and bore a hole through it 3 inches from the top. Bevel the top so that the gate will pass over it, and it will then fall back and hold the gate open. When one's hands and arms are full of things, as they often are on a farm, it is a great convenience to have a gate or door held open automatically. No simpler or more effective device for the purpose can be found. A similar device can be adapted to use as a latch to catch and keep a gate or door closed.

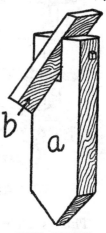

GATE CATCH

## GOOD BARS FOR THE FARM

It is an important matter to the farmer that his farm should be well equipped with good, substantial bars. Some farmers go to as much trouble in a year's time in moving a poor gate or bars back and forth as they drive in and out of fields, and in chasing cattle about, as making dozens of such bars as are represented here. Use round poles about 2½ or 3 inches in diameter. Set two good-sized posts one on either side of the barway, and to each one, an equal distance apart, nail large horseshoes, al-

lowing the round part to stand out far enough from
posts to admit the bar poles easily.

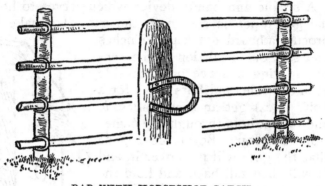

BAR WITH HORSESHOE CATCH

## DURABLE FLOATING FENCE

This is a cheap and easy way to make a good,
strong cable on which to hang a water gate, when
it becomes necessary to have a fence cross a stream:
Set two good, large posts about 3 feet deep in the
ground and about 6 feet from the banks of the
stream. ·Get a piece of wire (barbed wire will do,
but smooth wire makes a much better looking job),
long enough to go from one post around the other
and back again about six times, being careful to
fasten each end securely at the proper height from
the ground. Then get a strong piece of wood about
1 x 3 inches and about 4 feet long, stand as near the
middle of the space between the two posts as possible, and place the stick between the two sets of
wires. Turn around until all the wires are well
twisted together, being careful not to twist too much.

On withdrawing the stick, the wires will only
untwist two or three times. After the gate is hung,
the stick may be again inserted in the same place

and several more twists given to take up the sag caused by the weight of the gate. Then fasten one end of the stick to the top of gate and it will be im-

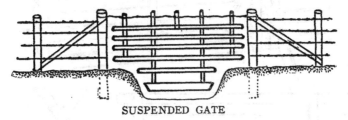

SUSPENDED GATE

possible for the cable to untwist any more. This has been found to answer all the purposes of an expensive cable and looks and lasts just as well.

## FENCE ACROSS A STREAM

To construct a fence across a creek or small stream, set a post on each bank and brace well. If a tree happens to be near at the right place, so much the better. Then fasten wire securely on posts, leaving enough slack so a weight in the middle will draw the wires toward the bed of the stream, thus making it impossible for stock of any size to get through. A large stone makes a good weight. It can be blocked up to desired height and fastened in position with smooth wire.

## TEMPORARY SHEEP FENCE

One of the best portable fences for use in soiling sheep is made in panels with supports, as shown on next page. Panels are 10 feet long, made of 4-inch board solidly nailed together. After this fence is once put up, sheep are not likely to overturn it. A fence 3½ feet high will turn most flocks.

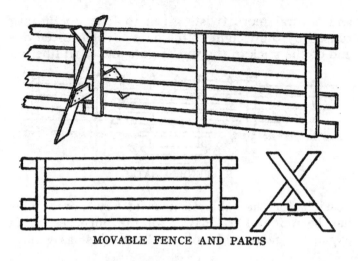

MOVABLE FENCE AND PARTS

## FASTENING HEAVY DOORS

There is little difference in the effectiveness of these two locks for heavy doors. The left-hand

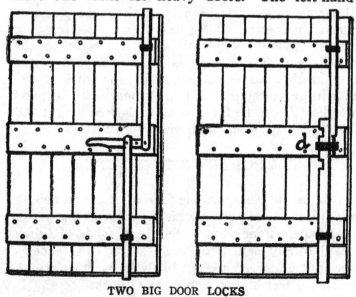

TWO BIG DOOR LOCKS

device is extremely quick and handy; the other very neat and substantial. The lock to the left has both bars pivoted to a lever handle, which is pivoted to the door midway between the ends of the arms. Moving the lever handle up moves both arms out of slots above and below the doors. The fastening may be also worked from the inside by cutting a slot through the door and setting a pin in one of the arms, so that it can be moved in the slot.

The right-hand fastening is worked by raising the lower arm so that the notch incloses the middle staple at *d*. Then the upper arm can be pulled down. Both arms stay firm and snug whether the door is shut or open.

## HOLD THE BARN DOORS SHUT

A latch that will hold double doors shut is shown in the cut. This is put on the inside of the door that is closed first. It is made of hardwood 4

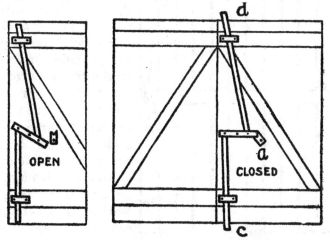

LATCH FOR DOUBLE DOORS

inches wide and 1 inch thick. To open the door, turn the piece, a, to the right and pull down on the crosspiece which is fastened to the door by a bolt in the middle. This will raise the latch, c, and lower the latch, d, as shown in the cut to the right.

Open your doors to a fine day, but make yourself ready for a foul one.

Prosperity is the thing in the world we ought to trust the least.

## FASTENING THE STABLE DOOR

A handy stall door fastener is shown in Figure 1. It consists of a piece of oak or other hard wood

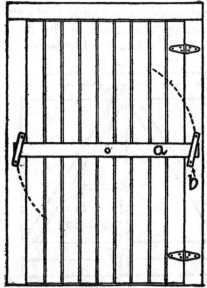

4 inches wide by ⅞ inch thick and 2 inches longer than the width of the door. It is fastened to the door by a ⅜-inch bolt through the middle and it works like a button. Cleats, b, are sawed out and fastened to the door jamb on each side to hold the fastener in place.

Another handy fastener that can be worked from either side of the door is

FIGURE I—LONG FASTENER   shown in Figure 2.

There are three upright pieces, *a*, two of which
are on the door and one on the door jamb or casings.
Another piece, *b*,
slides t h r o u g h
these and holds
the door shut. A
p i n, *c*, g o e s
through the bolt
and through the
door to open or
shut it from the
opposite side.
The bolt is kept
s h u t b y t h e
spring, which can
be made from a
piece of hickory,
or other t o u g h
hardwood, whit-
tled down to the
proper thickness.
The spring fea-
ture is the chief
advantage, and a

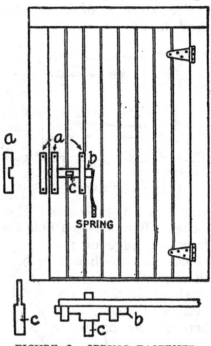

FIGURE 2—SPRING FASTENER

very important one it is, of this excellent fastener.
It is also a good point that the fastener works
nicely from the opposite side of the door.

---

Sell cheap and you will sell as much as four
others.

They must hunger in frost that will not work in
heat.

'Tis easier to build two chimneys than to maintain one.

## HOMEMADE DOOR LATCH

This consists of three pieces of oak or other good hardwood, as shown in the drawing. For

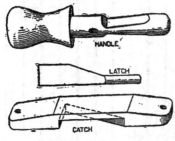

DETAILS OF LATCH

the handle use a piece 8 x 2 x 1 inches. Shape a flattish knob on one end 3 inches long. Work down the rest so as to pass through a 1-inch auger hole. Shape a knob on the other end by flattening the sides. The latch is made of a piece 5 x 1 x ⅜ inches. The catch is 8 x 2 x ¾ inches. Bore a 1-inch hole for the handle 3 inches from the edge of the door. Push the handle through the hole and mark on it the thickness of the door; then bore in the handle a ⅜-inch hole for the latch. Now assemble the parts according to the finished figure, which shows the latch thrown back. A little peg may be used to keep the latch from falling down when the door is open. By taking pains to shape and

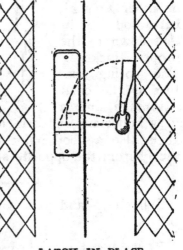

LATCH IN PLACE

finish this latch nicely it will look well enough to please the artistic eye of the most fastidious.

## IMPORTANT POINTS IN HOUSE BUILDING

 THE following points in building a house are considered of the greatest importance by a well-known architect: Carefully watch that the foundation walls are substantially laid, and accurately leveled on their upper surfaces, so that the doors shall not strike the floor or carpets in opening, nor the tables, chairs, or other furniture be obliged to stand on three legs.

The framework, when raised, should be plumb, so that all on or in the building can be cut square, and applied without tedious fitting. The siding should be thoroughly seasoned in the open air before using, and carefully applied with close joints, and well nailed. The edges of all water tables, corner boards, and window frames should be painted before setting.

The shingles should be carefully laid, breaking their joints at one-third of their width and double nailed. The flooring should be dry, close laid, and nailed with two nails to each beam. The partitions should be set with studding of selected width, and their angles or corners should be anchored firmly together to prevent the walls from cracking in those parts when finished. The chimneys should be carefully constructed, all points between the brickwork should be well filled with mortar to prevent sparks from passing through to the framework.

All mortar for plastering should be properly mixed, and allowed sufficient time (at least a week) for the thorough slacking of the lime, and a complete permeation of the caustic properties. Thin coats of plastering are better than heavy ones. A mortar that does not crack in setting or drying is sure to be good.

The interior wood finish should not be begun until the plastering is completely dried out, and all loose mortar is removed from the building. All woodwork usually painted should be primed as soon as in position.

## A VERY CONVENIENT HOUSE

The accompanying picture and plans show the outside and interior arrangements of a very convenient home built the past year by one of our

AN ATTRACTIVE HOME

agricultural editors. It is 34 feet wide by 30½ feet deep, with a 7-foot cellar underneath. The house contains 10 rooms, including two in the attic, besides a storeroom in addition to those shown. All the rooms are of good size and have two or more large windows, which make them light and sunny and supply plenty of good air.

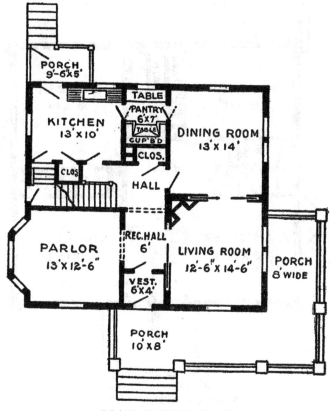

PLAN OF FIRST FLOOR

Economy of construction, as well as of doing the work, was kept in mind in the planning. The location of the stairs is somewhat unusual in a house of this sort, but is such that only one light

is necessary from first to second floor. There are
plenty of large closets on the second floor, which
are greatly appreciated.

The porch is not roofed except over the door, but

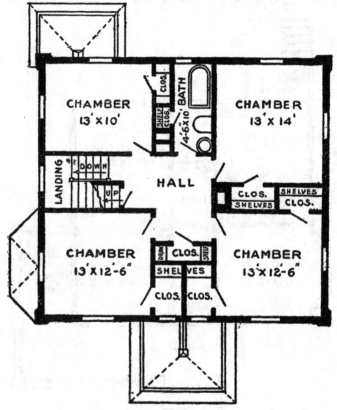

PLAN OF SECOND FLOOR

an awning, which is taken down in the fall, makes
it cool and shady in summer, and allows the sun-
shine to reach the living room in winter. The
first story is 9 feet from floor to ceiling, the second
8 feet and the third 7 feet 6 inches. The house

is piped with gas and wired for electricity, provided with the best quality of sanitary plumbing

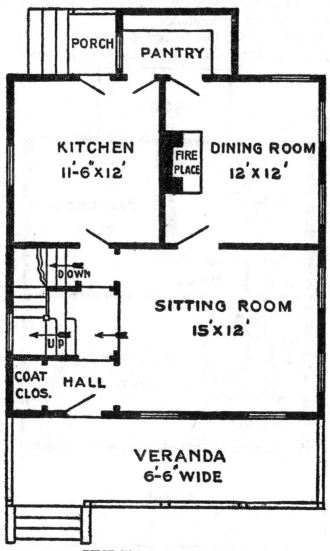

FIRST FLOOR COTTAGE PLAN

and heated with hot air furnace. A similar house can be built for about $4,000, more or less, according to finish and locality. Occupancy proves it to be a model of convenience.

If a bigger kitchen is desired, it can be obtained by going back farther. Many would prefer a

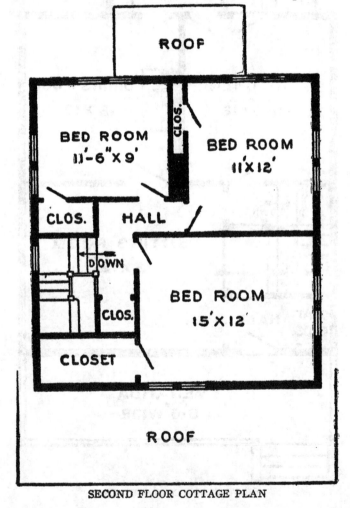

SECOND FLOOR COTTAGE PLAN

wider bathroom. A foot taken from the back chamber on the right would greatly improve the bathroom and still leave a large chamber. If desired, a large roofed piazza can be added.

## BUILDING A BLOCK HOUSE

A Kansas farmer needed a house on his farm, but had very little money. He found that only a little was needed for a cement block house. He ordered a cement block machine and bought 12 boards 10 inches wide and 12 feet long, which were cut in seven pieces of equal length. Two cleats were

$400 CEMENT BLOCK HOUSE

nailed on each, about 3 inches from the ends. These were for pallets and cost about 7½ cents each. The cement blocks were 8 x 9 x 18. As the block machine had no attachments, some contrivances were made for making half stone, three-quarter and others.

For caps and sills for doors and windows 9-inch boards were taken, using three for each mold, and

two holes 2 inches from the edges and 3 or 4 inches
from the ends of two of them were bored. Then
the farmer made cement blocks for the ends 9 x 8
inches, laid the other board on the ground, placed
one of the others on each side of it edgewise, put in
the end blocks, and through the holes put long
bolts and bolted it tight together. Then it was
ready to fill with concrete. These boards were as
long as were needed to make the caps or sills. A
sprinkler, sand shovel, plasterer's trowel, and a
wire sieve of ¼-inch mesh were obtained.

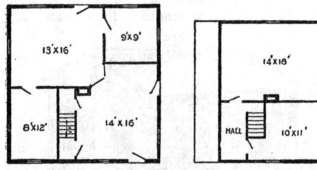

FIRST AND SECOND FLOOR PLANS

The sand cost nothing except hauling. The
machine was set up near a spring. A box something like a wagon bed with both ends out was
made of boards, the block machine placed in one
end and the pile of sand at one side. Three shovels
of sand and one of cement were placed in a tub
and mixed thoroughly. Then a boy took the
sprinkler and sprinkled it while another mixed,
until it was dampened evenly all through. Then
they spread 35 shovels of sand in the mixing box
and shook one sack of cement over it, which made
a five-to-one mixture. This was thoroughly mixed

by shoveling and sprinkling until it was good and damp, but not wet. This quantity made ten blocks.

A pallet was placed on the open machine, the machine closed, and some of the richer mixture of concrete placed on the face about 1 inch thick. The mold was then filled with the five-to-one mixture, while one of the boys tamped it, put in the core, and smoothed off the top with a trowel. The core was then carefully lifted out, the machine opened, and the pallet with the stone on it placed on a level piece of ground.

In three or four hours the blocks were ready to sprinkle. When 30 hours old they were placed on end and the pallets used for more stone. After standing for two days, during which time they were sprinkled frequently to keep them damp, they were dumped in the creek, where they were left until ready for use. The foundations were made by first putting into a trench about 6 inches of broken rock, then 4 inches of concrete.

The house is 26 feet square, the walls 12 feet high, with gables north and south. The picture of the house and arrangement of the two floors are shown in the illustrations. We used 12,400 pounds of cement, which cost 60c per 100, or $74.40. Doors and windows were brought at a cost of $33.75. Chimney, plastering and lumber for floors, roof, partitions and finishing, all of the best, cost $240. The hardware was $30, making the total cost of house $378.15, not counting cement machine or labor, all of which was done by the family.

---

Art imitates nature, and necessity is the mother of invention.—Richard Franck.

Consider the end.—Chilo.

## A PRACTICAL ROUND BARN

There is no economy in building a round barn, that is, strictly round. The barn here illustrated has 26 sides nearly 12 feet long, making a barn 94 feet in diameter. The sills, plates and roof in a strictly round barn are very expensive, and the work will not last as well as when built as shown. The floor space of the first floor is nearly the same as if round, and the hay loft is very little smaller. If the building is round, the walls should be lathed

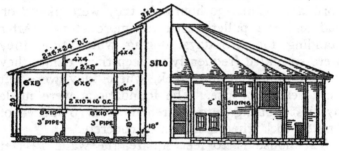

CROSS-SECTION OF BARN

with metal lath, over rough boxing, and plastered with two coats of portland cement. In fact, this finish is to be preferred in building any shaped barn, as it requires no paint and practically no repairs.

The floor plan of the barn shown is self-explanatory. It has stalls for 40 milch cows, three bull pens, two hospital stalls, pen for baby beef that will accommodate about 2½ cars of calves, stalls for seven horses, including the two box stalls, and the feeding room and silo. The silo is 16 x 34 feet, will hold about 140 tons of silage, and requires about ten acres of average corn to fill.

The hay loft has 166,500 cubic feet of space, and deducting the silo and bins for ground feed will hold 300 tons of loose hay. The ground feed is stored in hopper-shaped bins above the feed room, and drawn down through small spouts as wanted. The hay is handled with hay forks, and to locate

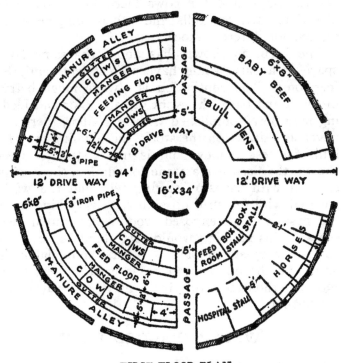

FIRST FLOOR PLAN

the trolleys as near the roof as possible, trap doors are left in the loft floor, and the hay hoisted from the driveways. A circle trolley may be installed, or two straight ones. Several large hay doors are also built in the outside walls above the loft floor. The silo, the floors of the cow stalls, including the gutters and mangers, also the 8-foot driveway around the silo, are of cement, and, while it is intended to install litter and feed carriers, it is also intended to drive around the entire barn, or the feed floor with a cart if desired. The interior arrangement of first floor may, of course, be changed in several ways, and the cows faced in the opposite direction, etc., or stalls and other equipment arranged for different stock.

The barn, as shown, has about the same floor space as a barn would have 36 feet wide and 180 feet long. The ventilation is always much better in the round barn, the work of caring for and feeding may be accomplished with less labor, there are never any drafts on the stock, the building may be built for less money, and is much stronger. As shown, the barn has a stone foundation, the roof is covered with asbestos roofing felt, and the walls covered with 6-inch drop siding. Everything is of the best, and all exposed woodwork painted two coats. This building would cost about $4700 without the cow stanchions. Where home labor is used, and the lumber can be secured for less than $30 per thousand, the barn may, of course, be erected for less.

## A WELL-ARRANGED BARN

This Kentucky barn has a frame of oak, 6 x 6 inches. Center posts 23 feet 9 inches; shed posts 16 feet tall; studding and braces 2 x 6-inch poplar; joists 2 x 10-inch poplar, oak and pine. The sheeting is of poplar, beech and ash. The bevel siding is select poplar. Cornice and base, white pine. All doors are two thicknesses, front is dressed cypress and the back dressed white pine. The lower windows are 10 x 12-inch, 12 lights and upper ones inside the building. The joists are set 20 inches from center to center. The loft is 8½ feet from lower floors.

The floor plan shows the arrangement as follows: Number 1, icehouse, 18 feet deep, walled up with stone; 2, carriage house, 16 x 18 feet; 3, stairs, leading to lumber room over carriage room; 4, corn

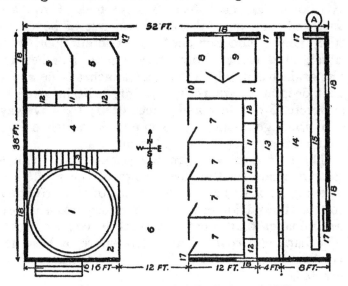

GROUND PLAN OF A KENTUCKY BARN

crib, 8 x 16 feet, over which are the grain bins for wheat and oats. These bins have chutes running down into the corn crib, from which grain is filled into sacks. Numbers 5, 5, are box stalls, 8 x 12 feet; 6, driveway, 12 x 38 feet; 7, 7, 7, 7, box stalls, 6½ x 12 feet; 8, harness room, 6 x 8 feet; 9, feed mixing room, 6 x 8 feet, with spouts running from cutting box and bran bins overhead; 10, alleyway running from driveway to feed alley; 11, 11, 11, hay

chutes, with openings near the bottom, 1 x 2 feet.
These openings are directly over the feed boxes and
any hay that falls while horses are feeding goes
into the boxes and none is wasted. Number 12,
feed boxes, 1 x 2 x 2 feet; 13, feeding alley, 4 x 38
feet.

Overhead at X is an opening from the hay loft
where alfalfa, clover, cowpeas and hay are kept for
the cows; 14, cow shed, 8 x 38 feet. Cows are
fastened with stanchions and fed out of boxes on
alley floor. The cow shed has concrete floor, with
a fall of 2 inches from stanchion to Number 15,
the drain basin, which is 1 foot 2 inches wide and 1
foot deep at A, where it runs into a basin made of
concrete, 6 x 6 feet and 2 feet deep; 16, driveway
into carriage room; 17, openings in which siding
doors hang when open; 18, windows.

The roof is of tin, standing seams, with Yankee
gutters made on the lower edge of the roof. An
opening 10 x 10 feet in the center of the driveway
loft is allowed for hay and other feed taken up by
an unloader that runs on a track in comb of roof.
The barn will cost about $1500—more or less, ac-
cording to cost of building material where it is
erected.

## A HANDY SMALL BARN

This barn is arranged to meet the needs of a
small farm. It can be built in most localities at a
cost not to exceed $500, and if a farmer has his
own timber, at even less cost. The outside dimensions are 36 x 48 feet, and it is 16 feet to the eaves,
with a curb roof. The stables should be about 8
feet high, which allows plenty of loft room above
for hay.

In the floor plan the cow stalls, A, can be made
of any width desired, 3½ feet being best for general purposes. At B are two large box stalls for
cows with young calves. The mangers, C, are 18
inches wide, with a rack for hay or fodder above.
At D is the feed room and alley, which is 8 feet
wide. At E are the mangers for the horses, with

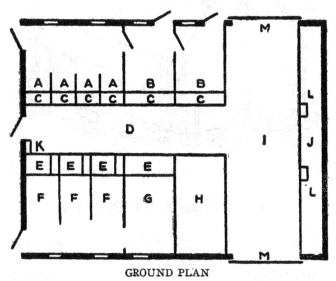

GROUND PLAN

a feed box at the right side. At F are three horse
stalls 4 feet wide, in which horses can be tied. At
G is a large box stall for mares and colts.

At H is provided the granary, which can be sub-
divided into bins as necessary. The portion I is
the driveway, which affords ample storage space
for tools, wagons, etc., and is used as a driveway
when hay is being elevated into the loft above.

There is a large corn crib, J, at the end, which
can be filled from the outside and emptied from
the inside. It is narrow and so arranged that the

corn will dry out quickly. Chutes from this bin should be provided at L. A ladder to the hay loft at K is a convenience which should not be omitted.

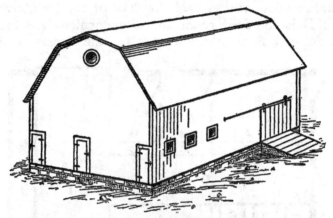

VIEW OF COMPLETED BARN

## THE FARMER'S ICEHOUSE

In a properly constructed icehouse, and when the ice is properly packed and cared for, no waste should take place from the inside of the pile of ice. The melting from the sides, bottom and top is caused by insufficient insulation. The waste from the bottom is generally the greatest. The amount of ice melted in the bottom of the icehouse varies from 1 to 6 feet during the year, depending upon the construction of the floor. If the icehouse is provided with an airtight floor, with the ice laid on at least 18 inches of dry sawdust, the bottom waste rarely exceeds 12 inches during the year; on the other hand, if the ice is piled in the icehouse on the bare ground without any insulation under it, or any provision made for drainage, the meltage fre-

quently is 6 feet.   The side and top meltage is not
so great, but it frequently ranges from 1 to 3 feet,
depending upon the insulation.

## Location and Building

The location should be where the ice can be removed and delivered with the least amount of labor;
however, it is very important that the icehouse
should be located in the coolest place, in as dry a
place as possible, and always above ground.   The
lowest layer of ice should always be at least 6
inches above the outside level of ground.

The size of the building must be determined by
the amount of ice used during the year.   For instance, a dairy farm upon which 35 cows are kept,
and from which the milk is sold, needs an icehouse
16 x 16 and 14 feet high.   If the cream is to be sold
and skim milk fed to the calves, immediately from
the separator, an icehouse 14 x 14 and 12 feet high
is of sufficient size.   In both cases we make allowance for the use of 25 pounds of ice per day during
the summer months for household purposes.   For
a man who keeps about 20 cows and sells the milk,
an icehouse 14 x 14 and 12 feet high is of sufficient
size; however, in no case should an icehouse be
smaller than 12 x 12 and 10 feet high, because the
outside surface is too great, compared with the
volume, and, therefore, too much ice is wasted in
proportion to the amount used.

The building should be as near the shape of a
cube as possible, for the cube contains the greatest
amount of volume with the least amount of surface
exposed other than circular forms.   It is not always practical to build as high as we build square,

owing to the amount of labor and the inconvenience of storing the ice; therefore, the dimensions given are really the most practical.

If the icehouse is not built upon a sandy surface and where rapid drainage is natural, it is

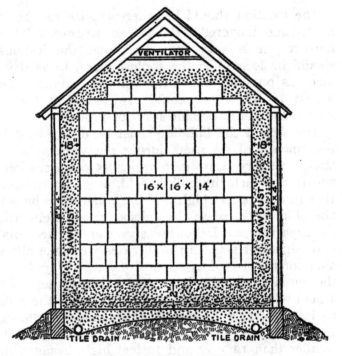

CROSS-SECTION OF ICEHOUSE

necessary to cut a space to a depth of 12 to 18 inches, where the icehouse is to be located, lay a tile drain to drain this, and fill it with sand or finely crushed stone. Put a 6-inch foundation of concrete of the size you wish to build your icehouse in this pit, and fill around the outside.

## Framing the Icehouse

The framework is made by laying 2 x 4-inch sill on the concrete foundation; fasten this to the foundation by cementing a few bolts into the concrete and allowing them to extend through the sill; 2 x 4 studding are then placed upon the sill, 16 inches apart from center to center. The rafters for the roof are likewise made of 2 x 4's, placed the same distance apart as the studding, but the purlin plate upon the studding should be at least 6 inches wide. The outside of studding may be boarded either with common sheeting and paper, upon which poplar siding is nailed, or with patent siding or ship-lap siding, the latter being the cheapest and requiring only a single thickness of board.

The roof should be made with not less than one-half to one-third pitch, and preferably covered with shingles, for shingles are better insulators than either slate or metal. Paper may sometimes be used to good advantage. A cupola or flue should be built upon the roof to allow for the removal of the warm air from the top of the ice. A ventilator may be placed in the gable end.

A continuous door should be cut in one end to allow the ice to be put in. This door may extend from the gable down to within 5 feet of the bottom.

Before putting in the ice place from 18 inches to 2 feet of sawdust or dry peat upon the floor. The ice should be harvested in regular shape, oblong, rather than square, and not less than 18 inches in width and 30 inches in length.

## Ice and Milk Houses Combined

The side elevation of an icehouse with milkhouse attached is presented in the drawing. It shows the

advantage of utilizing the water from the icehouse
for cooling the milk. No ice needs to be removed
from the icehouse. It operates automatically. If
the weather is warm the ice melts more rapidly and
keeps water in the tank at the required temperature.

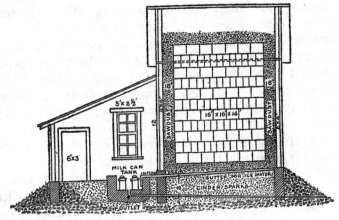

A GOOD COLD COMBINATION

## SMALL GREENHOUSES

The farmer who would make his crops of vegetables most profitable, or the small gardener who
would have an early supply of early vegetables for
home use or market must employ some kind of
glass structures to hasten these crops. The hotbed or cold frame have been much in use in the
past, but the cost of sash, shutters and mats is
nearly as much as the materials needed for a permanent structure, while the labor of caring for
cold frames or hotbeds is often much more than
that of the small greenhouse. In the latter one
may work with comfort no matter what the
weather may be outside. It requires much more
skill to run hotbeds successfully.

Small greenhouses may be built against the south side of the house or stable, Figures 1 and 2, or they may be built entirely away from other buildings, but the shelter of larger buildings on the north or west will be found of great advantage. If one has a basement to the house or stable, a lean-to house may be built, and heat from the open cellar in a large measure will heat the greenhouse in the mild weather of fall and spring.

## Material for Construction

A cheap and efficient house may be made by setting chestnut or cedar posts in the ground, covering the sides with lining boards, then two thicknesses of tarred building paper and sheathing

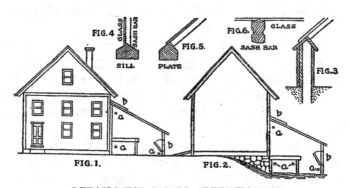

DETAILS FOR SMALL GREENHOUSES

outside, Figure 3. Cement, stone or brick will be cheaper in the end. The durability of glass structures will depend much upon the form of the materials. Clear cypress is now more used than any other material. Sills should be of the form shown in Figure 4. Plates may be made of plank as in

Figure 3, or as in Figure 5. Sash bars should have grooves along the sides to catch the drip from the glass, as in Figure 6.

The glass for ordinary work may be No. 2 double thick, large sizes, 16 x 20 inches or 20 x 24 inches, being much used. Smaller sizes will be cheaper in price, but more sash bars will be needed, and they cut off much of the sunlight. The glass should be put in with putty, made with about one-third white lead in it, and firmly tacked with triangular zinc tacks of large size, or the double-pointed tacks, which are so bent as to prevent the glass from slipping down.

## Set Glass in Warm Weather

Glazing should be done during the summer or early fall, as putty will soon become loose if frozen before well hardened.

In building there should be no mortises, but all joints be made by toeing in with long, slender nails. All woodwork should be thoroughly painted before fitting, and all joints filled with white lead paint. After all is done the frame should be painted before the glass is put in.

The most important and expensive feature of the small greenhouse is the heating. If one has a hot water or steam heater in the house, to which the glass house is attached, it will be a very simple matter to carry pipes through, as at *a*, *a*, Figures 1 and 2. Hot air also may be let into such houses, or a small kerosene heater in very cold weather may be used, if the house is built opening into the cellar.

Ventilators must be located as shown in Figures 1 and 2, at *b*, *b*. Very small structures may be run without much heat if opening into cellars or other heated rooms by having shutters or curtains to draw down at night and in very cold, cloudy weather.

## Covering with Hotbed Sash

Houses of small size may be made by building a frame upon which hotbed sash may be screwed. If one has the sash this is a cheap way of building, and such a house has the advantage that the sash may be entirely removed during the summer, but it is very difficult to make a close house with such sash.

The woodwork of greenhouses and hotbed sash should have a coat of thin linseed oil paint every second year. Much of the success to be obtained from any glass structure will depend upon the skill of the operator, and the thermometer, both outside and in, must be watched very closely. The temperature should be maintained as nearly as possible like that in the open air under which the plants grown thrive the best.

## WIRE FENCE CORN CRIB

In the drawing is shown a handy, inexpensive corn crib, which possesses several advantages not possessed by the ordinary slat corn crib. It is made on 4 x 4-inch posts, with pans at their tops, to prevent rats from climbing in. The sills are 4 x 4-inch, the scantlings 2 x 4, and 2 feet apart. The fencing is nailed to these on all sides, and the door frame is similarly covered. The roof is made wide, so as to shed all possible water. The height, length

and width may suit the farmer's convenience. A
convenient width is about 5 feet at the floor, widen-
ing to 7 feet at the eaves. Owing to the very open

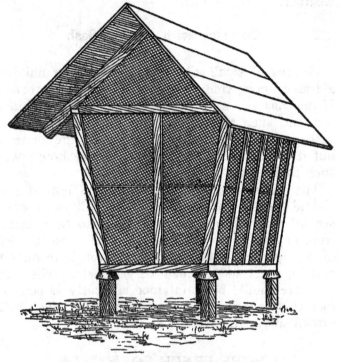

THE CORN CRIB

nature of this crib, corn dries more quickly than in
a slat crib, and as there is less chance for water to
lodge in the cracks, the crib will be more durable
than if built entirely of wood.

Want of cure does us more damage than want of
knowledge.

## HOW TO LAY A FLOOR

To lay a floor or board ceiling just right, and do the work fast, use a good lever, as in the illustration, taking for the supports two 1 x 4-inch pieces as long as the width of the room. The upright arm is 4 feet long with a hole 4 inches from the l o w e r

FLOORING LEVER

and through which it is pinned loosely between the ends of the supports. With a little practice, a good carpenter's job can be done on floor or ceiling.

## AN INEXPENSIVE VERANDA

A vine-covered veranda is a great comfort, but in many cases the expense seems greater than the owner of the plain little farmhouse feels able to stand. A farmer in Arkansas wanted one, and he set to work in this fashion. First he went to the woods and got a load of straight poles about 1½ inches in diameter and from 8 to 12 feet long. He next procured a number of nice, smooth boards for the flooring of the veranda, making it about 6 feet wide and 10 feet long and strengthening it with the necessary timbers. He securely nailed the poles about 8 inches apart around the flooring to form an inclosure, leaving an opening in front about 5 feet wide.

The poles in front were 7 feet from the floor to the roof and 12 feet at the house. About midway of their height the poles were straightened by a row

of poles nailed horizontally and another row was
placed at the top. To make all secure against rain,
the slanting roof poles were next carefully covered
with overlapping rows of bark. All this required
but small outlay of cash and even less of work. It
was then ready for the vines.

Being in haste for immediate results, the builder
planted some roots of the hard native woodbine,
which will soon cover any space with its rapid
growth. It is an easy matter to sow seed of the
morning glory, hardy annual gourd, or any one of
several hardy climbers and the result will soon be a
mass of shade and lovely blossoms besides, all of
which makes the summer evenings pass far more
pleasantly.

## CONCRETE ON THE FARM

The progressive farmer must not overlook the
economic value of portland cement concrete. Today is the age of concrete. It is crowding wood
and steel into the background, and bids fair to
become the most universal of building materials.
Concrete is extensively used by the largest land-
holders, and can be used by the men of more
moderate means to equal advantage. It is to be
recommended for general use by reason of its
durability, sanitary qualities and moderate cost.
Molded solid, it has no joints nor seams to afford
a lodging for dirt and foster the growth of noxious
fungi; it can be swept, washed, scrubbed and
scalded, without injury to its texture. Further, it
does not possess the disagreeable quality of absorb-
ing gases and odors. Add to these qualities, coolness in summer, warmth in winter and we have one

of the most logical building materials in present-day use.

Concrete is not expensive when compared with other materials of construction, such as stone, brick and wood. To be sure, the initial cost of wood is less than that of concrete, but when we consider the life and quality of the finished product, concrete is easily cheaper than wood.

Portland cement of the most approved brands costs about $1.60 per barrel, 1¼ barrels of cement being required for each cubic yard of concrete. Sand and gravel may be had from the farm or bought nearby at 10 cents a load. Add the cost of the forms and the labor of mixing and laying the concrete, which should be done at an expense not exceeding 75 cents per yard, and we have a total expense ranging from $2.75 to $3 per cubic yard, but under very favorable circumstances the cost may be reduced close to $2. Experience both in practical work and in the laboratory has proved beyond a doubt that the best brands of cement, as in all other goods, are the cheapest in the end, and should be insisted upon by all prospective purchasers. Atlas, Alpha, Saylor's, Edison and Giant cements are among the leading brands. The sand should be clean, coarse and sharp and free from all foreign matter that would in any way tend to weaken the concrete. Broken stone with sand and cement makes an ideal mixture, but it is objected to on account of the cost of the broken stone. Gravel may be substituted for the stone, however, with excellent results. The gravel should be washed and cleaned, and, if very coarse, passed through a screen. The gravel should range from ¼ inch to 2½ inches in diameter, but should not exceed 2½ inches and to obtain the very best results the major portion should be between the limits of 1 and 1½ inches.

## MIXING THE CEMENT

In mixing concrete for general use the following proportions are perhaps the best: One barrel cement to 3 barrels sand and 5 barrels gravel. In this mixture the spaces between the stones are entirely filled and when hardened the concrete virtually becomes a solid monolith.

To secure the best results mix the concrete as follows: Have the gravel washed and in readiness, usually on a platform of planking or boards, to permit easy shoveling and insure against waste. Add enough water to the cement and sand, which have been thoroughly mixed in a mortar bed, to make a thin mortar, not too thin, however, to permit easy shoveling. Spread the mortar on the gravel and thoroughly mix by turning with shovels. Then, without delay, shovel the batch of concrete into the forms or spread it on the floors as the case may be, being careful not to exceed layers of 8 inches at each filling. Each layer must be tamped and rammed till water flushes to the top.

Proceed in this manner till the forms are filled. In hot weather damp cloths or boards should be placed over the top of the concrete to keep it from checking after the final layer has been placed in the forms. The forms must necessarily be water tight and the concrete worked back from the boards with a spade, so the softer material may flow to the outside and insure a smooth surface. If this last is not done holes will surely result and the work will be disappointing. Let the concrete rest four to six days before removing the planking, concrete being somewhat brittle until thoroughly hardened, and while in the "green" state easily broken.

## MAKING CONCRETE BLOCKS

Concrete building blocks are ideal as building material on the farm. The cost to purchase these blocks has been beyond the reach of the farmer who desired to use them for all purposes; but by the use of the simple machine or mold described anyone can make the best quality of hollow concrete building blocks at an average cost of less than 6 cents each, the mere cost of sand and cement.

As the standard size block is 20 x 8 x 7½ inches, instructions are given for making the machine to build that size, but it can be constructed to turn out any size of block by changing the dimensions accordingly.

Take two boards 20 inches long by 7½ inches wide and 1 inch thick. These are for the sides. For the ends use lumber 10 inches long by 7½ inches wide. Care must be used to have the boards free from large knots and with an even grain, so as to avoid warping.

The above four boards were joined at three corners with six hinges; two hinges at top and bottom of each corner. In putting together have the two end boards set up against the sides as shown in Figure 1. At the fourth corner place a strong hook and eyelet to hold the machine together when making block, and by unhooking this allows the machine to be folded back away from the finished work, etc.

This makes a mold or form that is, inside measurements, 20 inches long, 8 inches wide and 7½ inches high, with top and bottom open.

For the core, take two boards of 1-inch lumber, cutting them 13 inches at the top and slanting to

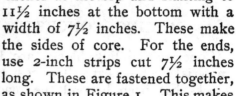

11½ inches at the bottom with a width of 7½ inches. These make the sides of core. For the ends, use 2-inch strips cut 7½ inches long. These are fastened together, as shown in Figure 1. This makes a slanting box which is set inside of

FIGURE I—CORE

the machine, as illustrated in Figure 2, and forms the hollow in the block. To the top of the core a round stick is fitted into place the length of the core, so it will set down level with the top for a handle to lift the core from the block when operating the same.

## To Operate the Machine

First set it on a board somewhat larger than the machine, as shown in Figure 2. This makes the bottom of machine and holds the block until dry. Enough of these boards must be provided for the

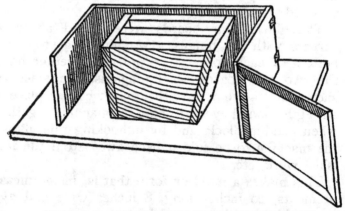

FIGURE 2—CEMENT BLOCK MACHINE OPEN

blocks made each day. Close the machine and fasten catch, then set the core in the center and fill the space around the same with the concrete mixture, tamping it in thoroughly. When full level off the top with a flat stick and carefully lift out the core, setting it on another board ready for the next block, unhook the catch and fold the machine back away from the finished block and you have the completed block ready to dry and cure. This method requires no handling and so has no danger of breaking while the block is yet "green," as it remains on the board or "pallet" until dry enough to be piled up, which they will be in three or four days.

When the blocks are to be laid in a side wall, between corners, take two 1½-inch strips 7½ inches long and attach with screws to the center of each end of machine on the inside. This molds a groove in the block, which is filled with mortar when laying the block in the wall and so securely ties it. By fastening with screws these strips can be easily removed when molding corner blocks.

### Blocks of Different Shapes

A neat panel block can be molded by taking the common half-round strips, cutting to the right lengths and fastening to the outside of the face of machine, as shown in Figure 1. For corner blocks they can be attached to either end of machine. By using small screws these can be removed when not desired and also enable you to panel either right or left end of block as needs require.

For making half-size blocks, have a piece of board that is exactly 8 inches wide and 7½ inches high, or so it will just fit into machine when core is removed. Set this in place in the middle half-way between the ends and fill with material. This will make two half-size blocks for use in breaking joints when laying wall. If desired to have these hollow, two small cores of proper size can be made to set in place when molding blocks of this size.

Rock face effects can be produced very easily by taking a 2-inch plank the size of the face of machine or the end as desired. On this draw a border 1½ inches all around, then take several irons, heat them red-hot and burn out the center in irregular shape, at least 1¼ inches deep. By making ridges and hollows in this burning process of different depths and as broken as possible, you will secure a face plate that will mold a very excellent imitation of a rock face. This, of course, can be made to suit any fancy.

One may follow the practice of making several faces and ends from plain and panels down to different rock effects, having these extra face plates the same size as given for the machine above. Then by using hinges as used on doors or any pin hinge, you can easily change the style of block by putting one face plate or end on machine in a moment's time. One machine can thus be used for any style of block and a great amount of time be saved in changing from one style to another.

This machine, in addition to being simple in construction and operation, is very rapid. With but little practice one man can make from 75 to 100 blocks daily and have each one perfect, as he does not break any by handling them after they are molded

---

According to her cloth she cut her coat.—Dryden.

## ANOTHER STYLE OF MOLD

All the lumber necessary to make this mold should be selected white pine or hardwood, free from knots and sap. The platform on which this mold rests should be 14 x 24 inches and be well battened together. The sides are made as shown

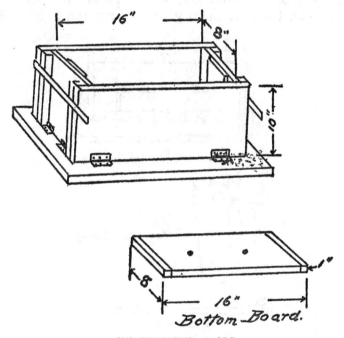

THE FINISHED MOLD

by the drawings, with a cleat on each end, which overlaps the end pieces and holds them in place. Both ends and sides are fastened to the platform as shown, with hinges, which permit them to be turned down to take out the completed block.

On each end is placed a flat iron bar with a notch in to fasten the whole mold together. These

bars are the same as hooks, only tne ends are pro-
longed to act as handles for convenience.

## Regulating the Height of the Blocks

The bottom board is intended to be fitted in the
bottom of the mold loosely and should be blocked
up from the bottom to give the required height of

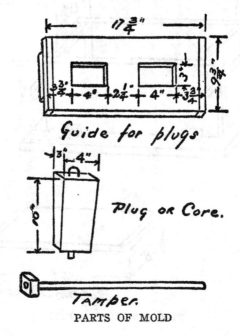

PARTS OF MOLD

the finished block. The end pieces of mold have a
thin piece of board running up and down to form
a key between blocks and should run down to top
of bottom board.

The plugs are made as shown, with a taper both
sides, so that when they are removed they clear all
the way out. The pins in the bottoms of the plugs

are to fit in the holes in the bottom board, which will steady them and hold them in place.

When the plugs are removed the board with the two square holes is placed over the top of mold and the handle of tamper is run through the rings in top of plugs and they are lifted up. This board is used as a guard and prevents the block from being broken when plugs are removed, and should not be used until the block is finished and ready to take out of mold. The tamper is made of a large iron nut and a piece of iron rod about 18 inches long.

### Filling the Molds

To make these blocks use one part of portland cement and three parts of good sharp sand, mix well and put enough water on to simply dampen the whole. Now close up the mold, put plugs in place, fill the mold one-fourth full and tamp down hard. Repeat this until the mold is filled. Scrape off surplus material, remove the plugs, then turn down sides and lift out finished block which is to remain on the bottom board until hard enough to lift off.

It will be necessary to have a number of these bottom boards. After a number of blocks are made they should be sprinkled from day to day for from 15 to 20 days to properly cure them before using. A barrel of cement will make about 50 blocks and one man can make a block in 12 minutes.

## MIXING CEMENT FOR BRICK

Many have found mixing the sand and cement the hardest part of cement brick making. An old vinegar barrel may be put to use by placing a grind-stone crank on one end and a pinion on the other. Two strong posts are set in the ground and the barrel hung over two pieces of round iron driven into the posts. A square hole is cut on side of barrel and covered with a piece of sheet iron hinged and a bottom to fasten.

The sand and cement are dampened, shoveled into the barrel and a boy may turn the crank. The mixing is done as fast as two men can mold, with a boy to sprinkle the brick to prevent drying too fast.

## REINFORCEMENT FOR CONCRETE

For heavy construction work involving beams and columns, reinforcement with steel rods is needed. Reinforced concrete is rapidly coming to be the most approved kind of construction of large

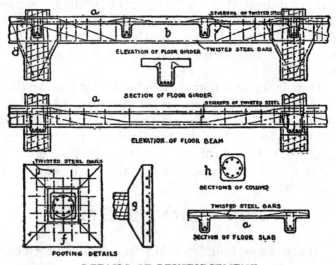

DETAILS OF REINFORCEMENT

buildings. Our own great building is one of the most noteworthy examples, being of reinforced concrete throughout. For any building where reinforcement seems desirable the following details will be found useful:

Plan of the footing or foundation of each column is shown in *f*; *g*, side view of footing and part of column above. The steel rods that run up through column are shown by dots in *h*, and the wire spiral by diagonal lines in *g*. *h* is cross-section of column filled with cement, the shaded part being the concrete. *a*, section of floor slab, 4½ inches thick; it is also shown on top of the floor girder and floor beam (crossbeams between girders). *b*, girder; *c*, cross-section of girder, the dots showing twisted steel bars that take up the tensile stress—compression stress is carried by the concrete. The steel bars, *d*, stuck into the column at an angle, are to prevent the girders from breaking off or "shearing" at column.

## MAKING A FROSTPROOF CELLAR

Some farmers build their own concrete cellar walls and chimneys with inexperienced help. Lay out your foundation the same way you would for any building. Have outside line of excavation plumb. Then use 2 x 4-inch studs the length required. Point one end, drive in ground, on line of inside of cellar wall, brace top of stud by driving stake in ground, and nail brace to stake and each stud. You must make everything firm. Then take square edge boards and place horizontally against the studs. (See illustration.)

Do not try to go around the whole cellar wall, take one side at a time to the height of earth surface, but turn your corner. Pay no attention to outside, let the stone and cement push up against the earth. It is the best plan to finish the whole wall up to the earth surface line before making the elevation above the ground line.

Above the earth surface line do just the same on the outside as you have been doing on the inside, but now you must use boards and studs, as up to

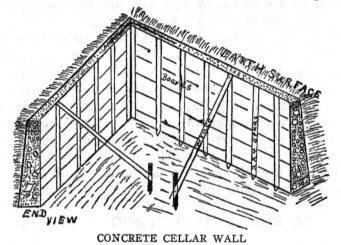

CONCRETE CELLAR WALL

this point the earth took the place of them. Plumb every stud you drive, and place them 24 inches apart. Have cellar window frames ready and place them as you come to them. Be sure and make extension for hatchway when building your main wall. For the corners use baled hay wire in wads, bending it around the center of wall, and a reinforced concrete corner will be the result.

Get cobblestones or any stone from the size of a goose egg to the size of your head, and put them in bottom of wall to depth of 1 foot. Make a mixing bed, say, about 12 x 36 x 72 inches. One man used an old wooden sink as near watertight as possible. Use one water pail of cement to three of fine gravel sand. Put one and one-half pails water in the mixing bed, then add the cement. Be sure and mix water and cement well before using sand. Throw sand in one shovelful at a time. Have one person mixing with a good-sized hoe, while another throws in the sand. Mix well.

Have it about the same as thin mortar, so it will leave the pail easily when pouring into the foundation. Cover the stones and then put in another lot and do the same to height of wall up to within a couple of inches. Do not put stones to full height of wall. To bring wall up to line, mix cement and water together (or one part sand and one cement) so it will run, and after wall is hard pour it on top and it will find its own water level and your sills will fit exactly. It is a good plan to have wall thicker at bottom than at top—perhaps 18 inches at bottom and 12 inches on top.

Now for hatchway steps. Put in the stones, as they save cement. Before the cement gets hard, drive in some large spikes, leaving them projecting about 2 inches on line of hatchway sills. Your hatchway doors will stay in place if sills are well-fitted on to spikes. One of the most important things is to be sure of the sand you use. If there is more than 10 per cent loam in the sand, your work will be a failure.

## A SUMMER COOL ROOM

A simple method of constructing a cool, outdoor cellar in localities where the common house cellars are too warm for use during the summer time, is shown in the accompanying sketch. It is a cellar made under the pump, so that the water pumped by the windmill has a very cooling effect. In places where it is difficult to obtain ice, it will prove indispensable to the dairyman who keeps a few cows. Another important item is the fact that a man does not have to pull up all of the pipes every

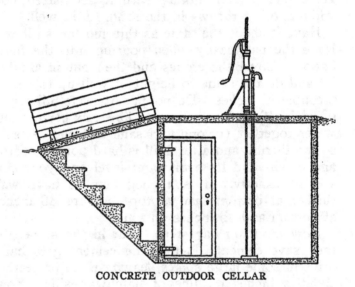

CONCRETE OUTDOOR CELLAR

time that he finds it necessary to repair the pipes and pump.

It is constructed of concrete. The top is reinforced with ½-inch steel rods placed 1 foot apart each way and the concrete work is about 6 inches thick. The sides are made by using a form, and the stairs are also made of concrete and are reinforced by small steel rods. The cost, including the labor, is about $50. In the west and southwest it will also answer the purpose of a storm cave, which is considered a fixture on all farms.

## A CONCRETE SMOKEHOUSE

The structure is about 8 x 10 feet and 7 feet high. It will keep the meat inside and thieves out. For a building of this sort 8-inch walls will be thick enough. Excavate to the proper depth below frost, which will be two feet or less, and use a mixture of one part portland cement, three parts sand and six parts gravel or broken stone.

Make the forms of matched boards, although square-edged boards could be used for this purpose. The forms must be well braced and may be raised as the work of laying the wall progresses. Space for a doorway must be left and two eyebolts inserted in the concrete for the door to swing on. The door jamb can be molded in cement if it is desired. An eyebolt for the lock and latch should also be placed in the wall.

The roof will no doubt be of boards or shingles. The plates should be placed on the concrete and held to it with bolts properly imbedded. An arched concrete roof can be made if desired, in which case it will be necessary to leave suitable vents in each end, or build a small flue to allow the smoke to escape. To make the house absolutely proof against fire a steel or iron door should be used.

## LAYING A CONCRETE FLOOR

A concrete floor should be level with the top of the sill, where there is much passing in and out with stock or wagons. There should be about 4 inches of concrete. If the earth is leveled off and tamped down hard, it would be unnecessary to put any crushed stone under the concrete in a building where frost or water does not get underneath. It is generally recommended to put several inches of stones, gravel or cinders on top of the earth, but many floors are laid without such a bottom. Partitions for horse stalls and cattle stanchions can be held in place on a cement floor by putting down iron belts or pieces of gas pipe when the floor is laid. Let them project 2 or 3 inches above the floor.

## MAKING A CONCRETE WALK

The best way is to dig a trench 16 inches deep, put in a foot of loose gravel or stone, leveling it off with fine material. On top of this spread 3 inches of concrete made of one part portland cement, two parts sand and four parts crushed stone or gravel. On this put a granolithic finish 1 inch thick mixed in the proportions of 1-2-3. Trowel it down smooth and hard. Joints ¼ inch thick and filled with sand should be left every 5 feet to prevent walk from cracking

## CEMENTING A CISTERN WALL

In making a surface waterproof, a mixture of about one part portland cement to two of sand will shed water from a roof or wall, but to make a surface perfectly watertight, so that it will keep out standing water, it is better to use neat cement only, that is, cement with no other material but the water with which it is mixed, and it will cost less to put on a coat ¼ inch thick of neat cement than one 1 inch thick, one-half or two-thirds sand, as the neat cement mixed with plenty of water is waterproof.

## SPECIAL USES FOR CEMENT

A sack of portland cement is a very useful thing to have for making quick repairs about the farm. A hole in a drain pipe can be stopped in a few minutes with a little cement, mixed with water, thick as putty. A crack in a barrel can be stopped this way. Hardwood floors may be patched and nail holes filled so they will not leak.

A waterproof floor can be laid over an old board floor in a short time. Sweep the old floor clean and dry and nail down all loose boards. Cover with a layer of heavy wire netting, tacking it down occasionally. Over this lay a layer of concrete of one part portland cement, three parts clean sand, mixed with water to a thin paste.

Smooth thoroughly, but if it is to be used by stock, brush with an old broom to make it rough, then let it dry thoroughly before using the floor. Gutters may be put in where necessary. Holes in an old shingled roof can be quickly stopped by forcing a little cement putty under the shingle where the leak appears.

Some special uses to which cement is being put are the making of bee hives, brick for pavement and ordinary foundations, cement shingles for roofing, grain bins in the form of square boxlike and round barrel-like receptacles. The use of this excellent material for farm structures is only just opening up and it is destined to become the most important material for general farm building.

---

A wooden reinforcement in the center of a concrete fence post is worse than useless. It does not make a bond with the concrete, and thus weakens, instead of strengthens, the post. Of course, the same is true of wooden reinforcement of any concrete work.

---

## A TIME-HONORED HANDY DEVICE

How dear to my heart are the scenes of my child-
    hood,
  When fond recollection presents them to view!
The orchard, the meadow, the deep-tangled wild-
    wood,
  And every loved spot that my infancy knew!
The wide-spreading pond and the mill that stood
    by it;
  The bridge, and the rock where the cataract fell;
The cot of my father, the dairy-house nigh it;
  And e'en the rude bucket that hung in the well—
The old oaken bucket, the iron-bound bucket,
  The old moss-covered bucket that hung in the
    well.

How ardent I seized it with hands that were glow-
    ing,
  And quick to the white-pebbled bottom it fell!
Then soon, with the emblem of truth overflowing,
  And dripping with coolness, it rose from the well.
                              —Samuel Woodworth.

## FREEZING ICE IN BLOCKS

WHERE a pond or stream is not handy from which to get the year's supply of ice, blocks can be frozen in forms with comparatively little labor. A supply of pure water is essential. The forms are best made of galvanized iron of any size desired. A convenient size is 16 inches wide, 24 inches long and 12 inches deep inside measure. The sides and ends should be made to taper ¼ inch, so

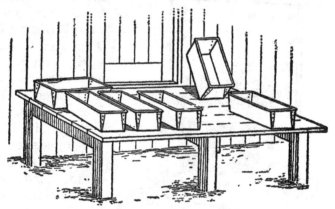

HOMEMADE ICE MOLDS

that the frozen block will drop out easily. The top of the mold should be reinforced with wire for the sake of strength and durability.

With a dozen or 20 forms one can put up quite a supply of ice during the winter. The forms should

233

be set level on joists or boards and placed a few inches apart. Fill them nearly full with pure water and let them freeze, which they will do in one or two days and nights in suitable weather. When frozen solid, turn the forms bottom side up and pour a dipper of warm water on them, which will release the cake of ice. The form can then be lifted off, the ice put away in the icehouse and the form filled with water again.

## SAVING THE SEED CORN

Here is a handy device for preserving select ears of seed corn. It consists of a wide board

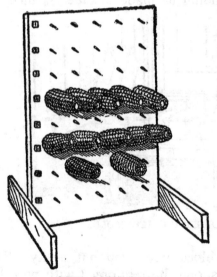

fastened between two supports nailed to the edges. The board stands upright on one end and may be as long as desired. Drive heavy spikes through it from the opposite side and stick an ear of corn upon each spike. This allows for the passage of air, and the ears can be examined without removing them from the rack. It

SEED CORN RACK

is much to be preferred to expensive wire racks, as each nail may be numbered and a record kept of the ears in this way. This rack was designed at the Idaho experiment station.

## RACK FOR SEED CORN

Here is a simple arrangement for keeping choice ears of seed corn. Take a 2-inch square timber for the upright, and make a solid base by boring a hole through the two base pieces, then drive the timber into it. Drive 4-inch spikes through the upright at intervals of 6 inches from four sides, and stick the ears of corn on these spikes by thrusting the same into the butt of the cob. Numbers may be placed above each spike, so that records can be kept of all of the corn. The corn should be placed on this rack as soon as picked and husked, and may be left there until planting time if the rack is placed in a dry room where rats and mice cannot get at it. A large post strongly mounted on a heavy pedestal may be used in a manner similar to the small upright described above. The bigger the post and the larger the

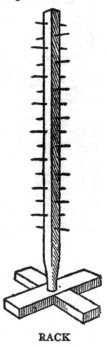

RACK

number of spikes used, the greater the capacity of the rack, of course. It is a good plan to make the pedestal heavy and strong in order that it may not be tipped over too easily.

---

The first years of man must make provision for the last.—Samuel Johnson.

Put your trust in God, my boys, and keep your powder dry.—Colonel Blacker.

## DRYING AND KEEPING SEED CORN

Never let it freeze before it is dry. Farmers have had seed corn exposed to a temperature of

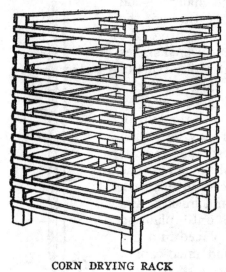

30 degrees below zero without injuring its vitality, and have had it ruined at 10 degrees above zero. We would not recommend kiln-drying for the general farmer, as this is only practicable where a grower is in the seed business. A very convenient way is to take four pieces 4 x 4

CORN DRYING RACK

6 feet long, set them up in a square, and nail laths on them two and two opposite. Leave a 6-inch space between the laths, so the corn will have plenty of ventilation. Lay your corn on this to dry, and if thoroughly dry it can lay there all winter.

———————

Knowledge is worth nothing unless we do the good we know.

It is better to give one shilling than to lend twenty.

Keep your mouth shut and your eyes open.

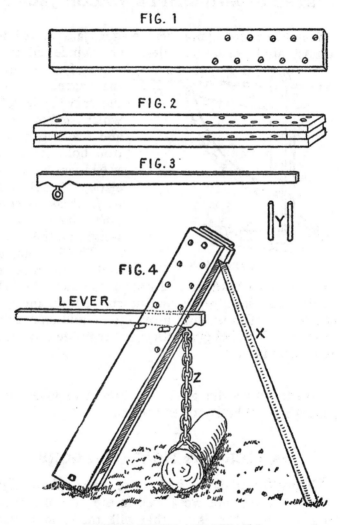

FIG. 1

FIG. 2

FIG. 3

FIG. 4

LEVER

WEIGHT LIFTER AND DETAILS

The drawings show the different parts and one of the many uses of this device.

## STRONG AND SIMPLE WAGON JACK

Here is a good, practical wagon jack suited to almost all kinds of vehicles. The whole thing is

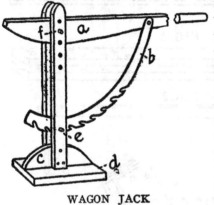

made of wood with the exception of the curved piece, *b*, which is of iron and hooks over an iron bolt, *e*. It is well to have a strong ½-inch bolt at *f*, so as to support the heavy weight on the lever, *a*. The bottom, *d*, and the piece, *c*,

WAGON JACK

are each 2 inches thick. In using the jack, the axle is lifted by simply pressing down on the handle of the lever. The teeth of *b* catch and hold on *e* automatically. The height of lever is regulated by moving *f* up and down.

---

Write down the advice of him who loves you, though you like it not at present.

---

## A JACK FOR HEAVY WAGONS

Many lifting jacks which are designed for light vehicles would not work well in the case of a heavy log wagon. Here is one that will stand a lot of hard usage and is simple and effective. Make the base and upright of heavy 2-inch oak plank and insert a ¾-inch bolt through the lever for a support. Have a good, strong hemp rope attached to the base, passing over the handle end of the lever, so that as it is drawn down and the wagon is lifted it can be hooked in a notch to hold it in position.

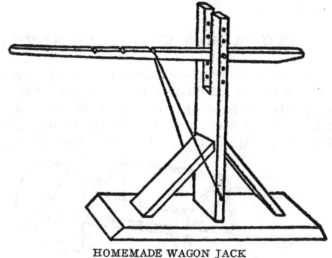

HOMEMADE WAGON JACK

## A CHEAP WHEELBARROW

The construction of this barrow is very simple. Get a pair of old plow handles, two gate hinges about 1 foot long, and a wheel, which may be found at the junk dealer's. The legs of the wheelbarrow

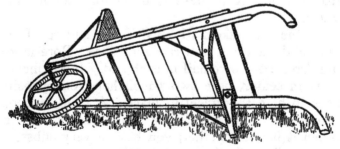

MADE FROM OLD MATERIAL

are those of an old chair, braced with a piece of iron. These articles in themselves are worthless, but in their combination we create something very useful.

## A WHEELBARROW CHEAP AND STRONG

Here is a picture of a handy, strong wheelbarrow that any farmer can make on a rainy day. Take a dry-goods box 30 inches long, 24 or 26 inches wide and 20 inches deep, and two sticks 5½ to 6 feet long and 3 x 3½ inches for handles. Nail or screw

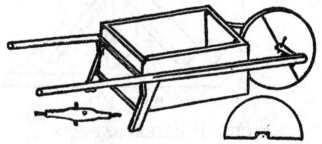

BOX WHEELBARROW

on crossbrace in front and rear, and pieces with brace as shown for legs. Cut four half circles from inch hardwood board and a notch in center to fit around axle. Nail these securely together for the wheel.

For the axle, take a stick 3½ inches square. Trim and band each end or wrap with wire. Bore holes and drive a 6d. wire nail in each end. Just 2 inches apart in center, bore two 1-inch holes on opposite sides to hold the wheel in place. A band of hoop iron around the wheel will make it last longer. When it is put together, you have a very substantial wheelbarrow that cost but little.

## HOW TO HANG A KETTLE

Using stones for a kettle support seems handiest oftentimes, but let the heat crack one of the stones and tip the kettle over, as it frequently will, does not tend to improve a man's language, let alone the loss sustained. It is much better to make a support such as is presented in the cut. The three uprights, of suitable length to correspond with the size of the kettle, may consist of any good wood. Through the top of these a hole is bored for the bolt to hold them together, which

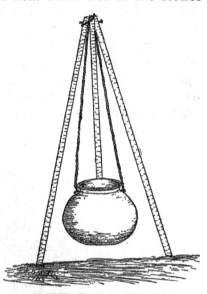

TRIPOD-HUNG KETTLE

must be long enough so they will have play to set up easily. All that is necessary then is to suspend two chains from the top and letting them extend downward to the proper distance, attach the ears of the kettle into the hooks on them. When not in use, the device can be folded together and laid away.

## A SNOW PLOW

No person not owning a snow plow can appreciate how useful one is after every storm. A horse, or if the snow be a heavy one, a span or a yoke of cattle and this simple homemade arrangement, and in less time than is required to tell it there is a path, and no back-breaking work either. It is only a big V braced so the snow is pushed both ways by it. It must be made of 2-inch planks at least 1 foot wide and not less than 6 feet long. If shorter it wobbles and does not stay on the ground well.

To make a good road for teams, chain it to one side of the wood sled and drive up and down. It spreads 2 feet, and will make your farm front look as if somebody of pluck lives there. For footpaths draw it from a ring at the top of the front so it will root.

SMOKEHOUSE SUBSTITUTE

## TEMPORARY SMOKING DEVICE

If one butchers only once a year it is not necessary to build an expensive smokehouse, for almost as good results can be obtained from a device such as that shown on page 242. It is made by taking both ends out of a barrel and mounting it upon a box or above a fireplace in the ground. The meat to be smoked is hung from the sticks laid across the top of the barrel, the fire built underneath and the lid put on.

## HOMEMADE HEATER AND COOKER

A cheap and economical heater may be of home construction. Make a frame of 2 x 8-inch pine 7 feet long and 27 inches wide. Put a bottom on

TANK AND COOKER

this of No. 18 galvanized iron, letting it project ½ inch on each side and 14 inches at one end for a stovepipe fitting. Spike the frame together and cover the corners with heavy tins to prevent any leaking. Nail the bottom on with two rows of nails.

Make a fireplace on the ground of stone and blue clay or brick and cement of mortar if preferred, 2 feet wide by 3 feet long and 18 inches high. Pile up dirt 1 foot high and 3 feet wide at the end of the fireplace for a flue, put stone on the earth the length of the galvanized iron, place the tank on this foundation and bank it up with dirt. In cutting a hole for the stovepipe, turn up strips of the galvanized iron for a collar, then drive an iron rod into the ground, put on two lengths of stovepipe and wire it fast to the rod.

A piece of sheet iron should be set up before the fireplace to control the draft and keep the fire. Such a heater, on one farm, is located near the windmill and storage tank and can be filled from either. The water can be heated quickly with cornstalks, straw, cobs or brush. One may boil pumpkins and small potatoes for fattening the pigs, and cook ground feed by pouring scalding water on the meal in barrels and covering with old blankets or carpets. A light fire will take the chill from ice water for the milch cows.

## USE FOR A TOUGH LOG

Most farm wood piles have two or three old logs lying about which nobody cares to tackle with an ax or blasting powder, and are too short for the sawmill. If straight, they will make good water troughs. Square the ends, mark off about 10 inches from each end, chop out the inside and trim the edges. An inside coat of oil or pitch tar will increase wearing qualities.

## A HANDY WOOD SPLITTER

For splitting wood a farmer in eastern Massachusetts uses a device as shown in the cut. Take a 2 x 8-inch plank about 3 feet long and an upright of the same material about 20 inches long. Set this upright at an angle of 20 degrees and use a brace of

WOOD SPLITTING DEVICE

the same material. The sharp points shown in the cut are 40d wire nails. Set the wood against these spikes in splitting it.

## HOW TO SPLIT WOOD

Wood splits much more readily in the direction up from the root of the tree than when the blow of the ax is downward. In other words, to split a chunk place it upside down—contrary to the direction in which it grew. It is much easier to split by slabs than to try to cleave through the center. This means to split off pieces near the edge.

## A PULLING HAMMER

If you want to make your old claw hammer do more work and do it better and easier,  have the handle projecting a little beyond the head. You will find it much more convenient in drawing a nail, as it makes a right angle for pulling the nail without bending it to one side. It takes the place of a block and is always on hand and ready in the right place for immediate use. The handle is simply whittled a little more than usual and driven through to the required distance. Don't drive it through too far, but about as shown at *a* in the picture. If it sticks out too much, it will be in the way when driving nails. Whittle it off rounding, and give it a finished appearance.

## MOUNTING THE FARM ANVIL

To make a solid foundation for an anvil, build a form of boards 14 x 18 inches square at the base, 18 inches high, tapering to 8 x 10 inches at the top. Fill this mold with rich concrete and fix a bolt in the center of the top of it to fasten the anvil. Afterward, melted lead can be poured around the base of the anvil, completing a very nice pedestal.

## SORTING POTATOES QUICKLY

The sketch shows a homemade potato cleaner and sorter. It consists of a number of hoops to which are fastened ½-inch slats so as to make holes

1½ inches square. Two heavy pieces, *a*, are placed inside the cylinder to hold the axle, *b*, which extends entirely through the machine and is turned by a crank, *c*. The frame made is 4 inches lower at the opening end of the cylinder so that the potatoes will run through freely.

At the crank end is a hopper, *f*, into which the potatoes are poured. The cylinder is 2⅝ feet long

POTATO SORTER AND CLEANER

and 3 feet in diameter. It will not bruise the potatoes, and the dirt and small ones run through on to the floor or crate and the marketable ones run out at the open end of the cylinder into another crate. With one man to turn the crank and another to fill the hopper, from 700 to 800 bushels can be sorted in a day.

---

An indiscreet man is more hurtful than an ill-natured one; for as the latter will only attack his enemies, and those he wishes ill to, the other injures indifferently both friends and foes.—Addison.

## HANDLING POTATOES EASILY

A bushel crate is often more convenient to use in handling ear corn, potatoes or other vegetables

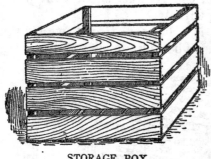

STORAGE BOX

than a basket. Crates that will hold a bushel when level full may be piled upon one another and thus stored in less space than baskets. At the same time they can be just as easily and just as quickly moved. They may be of light material. Pieces of wood 2 inches square are used for the corner posts. The slats may be made of ½-inch boards 3 inches wide nailed securely to the corner posts. There should be just room enough between the two upper slats so that the fingers can be inserted when lifting the box. The box will be more durable if the upper slats are an inch thick. A handy size for the completed box is 16 inches long, 14 inches wide and 12 inches deep, outside measurements.

## CUTTING SEED POTATOES

In the principal potato growing sections, medium to large seed is used for planting and cut to two eyes. In the famous Greeley district of Colorado, cutting is done by hand. Potatoes are shoveled into a bin or hopper, made of a dry-goods box raised on legs. The back is made higher than the front, so that potatoes will run down to the opening and the bottom is slatted to let out the soil shoveled up with the potatoes.

The cutting is simple. An old case knife, *a*, is fastened to the end of a plank or board, *b*, in such

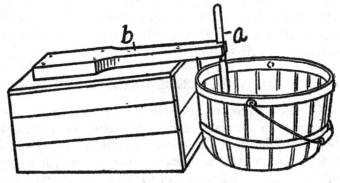

SEED POTATO CUTTER

a way that potatoes can be pushed against the knife and fall from it into the basket beneath. The operator sits on the box to which the board is fastened and can work very rapidly.

## ANOTHER SEED POTATO CUTTER

A wide bench is boxed in on both ends and one side. It is divided into two or three compartments, these being open in the front which corresponds to the side boxed in. To each of the compartments is attached a sack on hooks, and along one side of the bench in the middle of each compartment and right over the opening of the sack is fixed, in an upright position, a shoemaker's or common steel table knife.

Potatoes to be cut for planting are shoveled into the compartments of the box and in front of each compartment a man takes his position, being seated on a box or stool for comfort's sake. He seizes the tubers in rapid succession and by pulling them against the blade quickly cuts each one into as many pieces as desired; the pieces are then dropped into the open sack. It is claimed that by this indirect method of using the knife two fairly good cutters can cut each day all the potatoes ordinarily required for the use of one planter.

## HOW TO TEST SEED CORN

Of the different methods for testing seed corn, the most convenient and satisfactory is a shallow box provided with wet sawdust to furnish the moisture and a marked cloth on which to lay the kernels. The most convenient box is one 2 feet square. This will accommodate 100 ears. It is best to make it about 6 inches deep. Fill a sack half full of clean sawdust and soak it for three or four hours in water. Then spread this sawdust in the bottom of the test box to the depth of 1 inch. Take a smooth brick and pack the sawdust down all over the box, making it as level as possible. Be sure to get it packed firmly around the edges and in the corners.

Then take a piece of white muslin 25 inches square. Stretch this tight on a table so that it can be marked. Rule off on this cloth with a heavy blue pencil 100 squares 2 inches each way. Beginning at the upper left-hand corner number these squares in rotation from left to right. When the ruling is done, pack the cloth in the germination box so that it will rest firmly on the sawdust. This can be done by pointing the tacks in the edge of the box downward, and as the tack is driven in it will draw the cloth tight over the sawdust.

Of course, there is no advantage testing any ears that are of undesirable shape or conformation, therefore the first step is to pick out those nearest to the type wanted. Lay these out in rows upon a plank or upon the floor, separating each ten ears with a nail driven into the plank or floor. Starting at the left-hand end of the row call the first ear No.

GERMINATION BOX

1, then the first ear beyond the first nail will be No. 11, the one beyond the second nail No. 21 and so on.

Remove six kernels from ear No. 1 and place them in square No. 1 in the test box. Put six kernels from ear No. 2 in square No. 2 and so on through the row. In removing the kernels from the ear take a pocketknife in the right hand and the ear in the left. Place the blade at the side of the kernel you wish to remove and pry it gently. The kernel will come out easily and should be caught in the palm of the left hand. First remove a kernel from near the butt of the ear; turn the ear a quarter turn in the hand and remove a kernel from the center; turn the ear another quarter turn and remove a kernel from near the tip; another quarter turn and remove a second kernel from near the butt; another quarter and remove the second kernel from the center; another quarter turn and remove a second kernel from the tip. This makes six kernels from six different rows and representing the butt, middle and tip.

In placing the kernels in the box it will be found of advantage to point the tips all in the same direction, and also to lay the kernels with the germ uppermost. If the kernels are laid in the squares promiscuously, they may be thrown out of their places when the sprouts begin to grow. When the kernels are all in place, take a second piece of white cloth fully 24 inches square, moisten it and lay it carefully over the kernels. This will hold them in place while the top layer of sawdust is being put on. Take a third piece of cloth about 48 x 30 inches and lay it over the box so that the edges lap about equally. Then in this cloth put another inch of wet sawdust and pack it down firmly, especially around the edges. When this is done turn the edges of the cloth over the sawdust to keep it from drying out too rapidly and place the test box where it will not be subjected to cold below a living-room temperature.

### Reading the Results

After seven days carefully roll back the cloth containing the top layer of sawdust and lift the second cloth off the kernels. This must be done with care, because sometimes the sprouts grow through the cloth and the kernels will cling to it.

Observe the results in square No. 1. If all six of the kernels have vigorous sprouts, from ¾ to 2 inches long, you can be sure that ear No. 1 is thoroughly good. If in square No. 2 only two of the kernels have sprouted, you may know that ear No. 2 will make much better hog feed than seed corn. As soon as you have determined that ear No. 2 is really bad, pull it out from the row about half its length, leaving the other ears in place. After you have gone through the whole line, you may then go back and pick out the bad ears and discard them.

Of course, we would all prefer to use only those ears that gave a perfect germination, and if one has enough, that is the thing to do. But experience has taught that it is quite safe to use an ear, four of whose kernels grow strong sprouts. Or, if seed corn is scarce, one should not hesitate to use one that gave three strong sprouts and two weaker ones.

This testing may be done at any time after the ears are dry. It is generally more convenient to do it in winter, when there is not much outside work to be done. The box may be set behind the stove or any other convenient place, where it is sufficiently warm; in many cases, where there is an attic above the kitchen that room is a sufficiently warm place for testing.

Some put sand in an ordinary dinner plate, flood with water, and then drain the excess water off, place the seed on top of the sand, and cover with another dinner plate. Others use a saucer made of porous clay. The seeds are placed in this, the saucer set in a pan of water, and the pan covered.

These methods may be used for other grains as well as corn. In case of sowing grasses, alfalfa or wheat, it is often of great advantage to test the seed.

---

Every man has two educations—that which is given to him and the other, that which he gives to himself. Of the two kinds, the latter is by far the most valuable. Indeed, all that is most worthy in a man he must work out and conquer for himself. It is that that constitutes our real and best nourishment. What we are merely taught, seldom nourishes the mind like that which we teach ourselves.—Richter.

---

## KILLING INSECTS IN GRAIN

If one has not time to make a substantial box for fumigation of seed grain for insect destruction, barrels may be utilized for the purpose. Get two tight, strong barrels, such as coal oil barrels, and make water tight. Put in the seed to be fumigated, cover with a blanket and close-fitting cover. Before covering pour carbon bisulphide, which is explosive, over the grain, at the rate of 3 to 4 ounces for 5 bushels of grain. If it is not desirable to pour this poison on grain, set a saucer on it, and pour the poison in the saucer. Place a small block near the saucer to hold up the blanket 1 or 2 inches higher, lay blanket over the barrel, and place cover securely in place and weight with stone. This will kill the weevil in peas and beans.

## BINDING PINS FOR HAY

Every person moving hay ought to have a set of binding pins. They are made in a minute and serve an excellent purpose for a lifetime. The sketch shows a rope stretched over the top of a load of hay or straw. The upright pin is worked down into the load and the other twisted in the rope and turned around the upright until the load

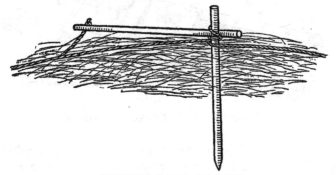

BINDING LOAD OF HAY

is tightly bound. Then a small rope that is kept tied in end of the horizontal pin is tied to the binding rope and the pressure is held. Each pin is 3½ feet long. One is sharpened and the other has a ½-inch hole bored through one end. Old fork handles are just the thing to make them of. One pin only may be made and a fork used to bind in the manner shown after the load is on.

---

Nothing is impossible to industry.—Periander.

## COMBINED DRAG AND HARROW

This road drag is all right. The front piece consists of a 4 x 4 oak strip, *b*, 10 feet long, through which are driven ordinary harrow teeth about 3 inches apart. This is attached to the rear piece, *a*, which is a 2 x 6 oak timber 10 feet long faced with

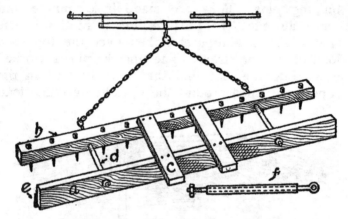

HARROWS AND LEVELS AT ONCE

3 inches of ¼-inch metal on the bottom, *e*, which projects 1 inch. These pieces are kept apart by wooden blocks, *d*, upon the bolts, *f*, and by the top strips, *c*, each 2 x 6. This makes a fine level road, as it harrows it and scrapes it at the same time.

## HOW TO HANDLE A ROPE

A rope is one of the most useful articles that are constantly needed about the farm; but too many farmers are not familiar with the many uses to which the rope may be put. The various sailors' knots may often be used to great advantage. To sling a plank for painting or other purposes make a bight of rope as shown in Figure 1, bringing the rope entirely around the plank, so as to prevent its turning and throwing the workman down. One-half to ¾-inch rope is usually sufficient for all practical purposes. A hemp rope is more generally used and stands wear better than other kinds.

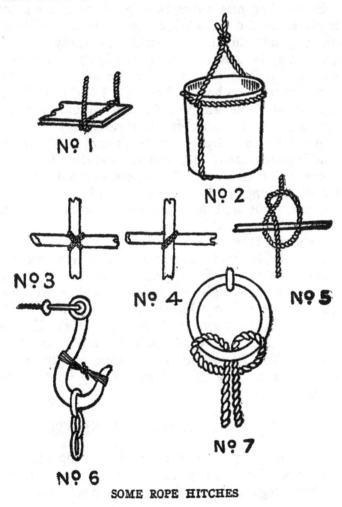

SOME ROPE HITCHES

A useful way to sling a can or pail from the end of a rope is shown in Figure 2. Prepared in this way the vessel is secure so long as the rope is not slipped off from the bottom. Secure the knot firmly at the top to allow no slipping and so that the pail may not become lopsided.

Scaffolding may often be erected by tying poles together as shown in Figure 3. This sort of lashing will not slip if made tight. In many cases a chain may be used as shown in Figure 4, in which case the weight should be on the side of the upright where the chain is lowest. All of these lashings must be drawn very tight so as not to allow any play, which may result disastrously.

An excellent hitch knot is shown in Figure 5, readily made, easily loosened and valuable for many purposes on the farm. This knot is readily untied by slackening up the drawing strand. It does not become tight and hard as many ordinary knots after heavy usage.

In many cases where heavy hooks are used they are liable to come unfastened unless a cord is affixed, as shown in Figure 6. A few turns of heavy twine or light wire in the middle will frequently prevent any loosening of the chain.

A ring hitch, shown in Figure 7, is a very effective and safe method, which may be made on short notice. The loose end of the rope is allowed to hang free or may be tied with a slip knot to the drawing strand.

## TYING SOME USEFUL KNOTS

A sailor judges knots for their holding qualities and also their ability to be quickly unfastened, without regard to the strain they have been sub-

jected to. A knot's main office is to hold, without
working loose or slipping, yet they do occasionally
fail absolutely to accomplish this, when made by
inexperienced hands. The accompanying diagrams
show some of the simpler knots that may be of
everyday use. In these, the mode of formation
can be readily discerned, because the rope's position is shown before tightening. The overhand
knot, Figure 1, is probably the simplest of all. It
is used only for making a knot at the end of a rope
to keep it from fraying or to prevent another knot
from slipping. If a slight change in formation is

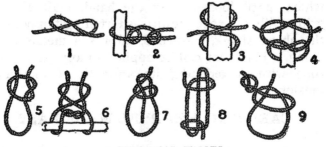

A FEW GOOD KNOTS

made, as in Figure 5, it develops into a slip knot or,
as it is sometimes called, a single sling, and its
purposes are obvious. A double sling is represented in Figure 6, and though it is slightly more
complicated, it is considerably more useful for any
purpose where a rope is to be attached to a bar or
beam and stand a steady strain.

Probably for convenience and emergencies no
knots equal the bow-line, Figure 7, because it will
not slip or give, no matter how great the tension;
in fact, the rope itself is no stronger, and the instant the strain ceases it can be untied as easily as

a bow.  When the end of a rope is to be secured,
the two half-hitches or clove hitch, Figures 2 and
3, are of great importance, for either of these bends
can be attached instantly to almost anything, and
their holding powers are exceeded by none.  The
square knot, Figure 4, can be used for infinite purposes, from reefing a sail to tying a bundle, the
advantage being, if made properly, of resisting any
separating strain on either cord, and yet can be
untied immediately by pulling one of the short
ends.

One of the best and safest slip knots is shown in
Figure 9, made with the overhand at the end,
which, until loosened by the hand, maintains its
grip.  When a rope requires shortening temporarily
the sheep shank, Figure 8, affords a means of so
doing.  This knot can be applied to any part of the
rope without reducing its strength of rectilineal
tension.

## CARRYING A BARREL MADE EASY

In the cities the ash collectors use a simple device,
which farmers might make and often find handy, as
barrels often become dried, weak and will not stand
rough handling.  The device is made of six pieces
of wood; four pieces are about 2 feet long and 4
inches in thickness and width.  Handles may be
whittled on one end of each.  About 10 inches from
the other end, boards about 2 feet long and 8 inches
wide are nailed as shown at *c, c,* in figure.  Pieces
*c, c,* are then cut in circular form so as to fit the outside of a barrel.

An old wheel tire may be straightened and four
pieces cut to be fastened to the ends of each of the
four handle pieces, as at *d.*  These are then riveted

together so as to make hinges as shown at *d, d*. The tire need be only long enough to fasten securely to the handle pieces. Of course, the blacksmith should drill holes in them, that they may be securely riveted.

To use this device, drop it over the barrel. One man lifts on the two front handles and another

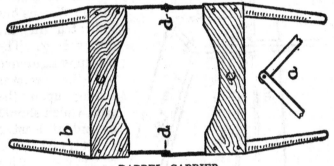

BARREL CARRIER

man on the rear handles. Boards *c, c*, close up in circular form, just beneath the lowest hoop round the upper end of the barrel, and cling tightly. The barrel is then lifted and readily carried without jar to its contents or straining the barrel. Of course, if all the barrels on the farm are of uniform size, the device could be made without hinges, and the barrels headed up could be rolled on pieces *c, c*.

---

The best part of one's life is the performance of his daily duties. All higher motives, ideals, conceptions, sentiments, in a man are of no account if they do not come forward to strengthen him for the better discharge of the duties which devolve upon him in the ordinary affairs of life.—Henry Ward Beecher.

## HARNESS CLAMP

The accompanying drawing represents a very handy harness mender which anyone who can use

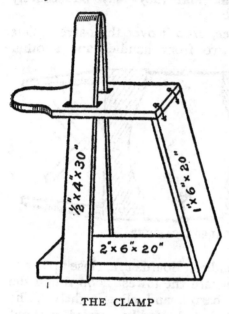

2"x4"x30"

1"x6"x20"

2"x 6"x 20"

THE CLAMP

a saw and hammer can make in a few minutes. It is made of lumber of the dimensions indicated in the d r a w i n g. The clamp is tightened by the worker sitting upon the seat, which should extend at least 2 f e e t f r o m the c l a m p s. The d r a w i n g shows the device with a shorter seat than that. It would doubtless be better to have the seat extended to twice the length shown from the left of the clamps and to have the base extended in a similar manner, so that the device will not tip over too easily. The joint at the upper right-hand corner may be hinged with heavy wire run through holes and twisted together underneath, or real strap hinges of iron may be attached.

---

They who provide much wealth for their children, but neglect to improve them in virtue, do like those who feed their horses high, but never train them to the manage.—Socrates.

## SUBSTITUTE FOR PIPE WRENCH

The drawing shown here illustrates a useful device for twisting pipe off or on its connections.
Three or 4 feet of new rope is frayed out at both ends, which are put together and wound tightly around the pipe to be turned, so that the first coil twists over the loose ends and continues around the pipe, two or three times, ending in a loop, through which a bar of iron is slipped, to be used as a lever. This simple plan will be found very effective in ordinary requirements for the pipe wrench, and is worth a trial. A more durable wrench may be made by using wire instead of rope. The loop

PIPE TWISTER

can be formed by closely twisting the ends of the wire with pincers. The rope is rather easier to handle because more flexible.

## MARKET WAGON CONVENIENCES

Farmers who regularly haul produce to market or deliver direct to customers will find the con-

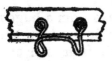

REIN CLIP

veniences described to be of much value. They save much time and considerable trouble and cost but little effort to make them. Instead of wrapping the reins about the whip, or letting them lie over the dashboard, a hook, such as shown in the first sketch, may easily be made of stiff fencing wire and secured to the top of the wagon or the dashboard.

Two other hooks may be arranged at the sides of the wagon to hold an umbrella, which would be kept there rain or shine, and never forgotten and left at home. This will save a drenching some time and perhaps some valuable produce.

Another convenience is a rear curtain of oilcloth stretched over a light board frame and hinged at

REAR SHADE FOR WAGON

the top, as illustrated. Two old stays from a buggy top will serve to support it, when it must be left open, and it will protect the driver from sun and rain while taking things from the wagon.

## CARRYING BUTTER TO TOWN

A refrigerator that one farmer uses in which he takes butter to town nine miles away in hot weather is made thus: Get two clean, tight boxes of some odorless wood, one 12 x 15 x 13 inches deep, and the other 9 x 12 x 10 inches deep. Slip one inside the other with a notched block in each corner to hold the inside box in place. Fasten the covers together so as to leave an air space of about 1 inch between them all around. The inner box will hold 20 pounds of butter nicely. It will carry butter solid in wagon all day in 90-degree weather.

## TO SHARPEN SCISSORS

Do you know that you can sharpen scissors, and easily, by passing the blades over glass jars? Take a bottle or jar, make believe you are trying to cut it (have one blade in and the other outside of the top of the bottle) and then allow the scissors to glide off the hard surface naturally, just as if you were trying to cut the glass. Use firm but not too hard pressure, and repeat the operation several times.

## HOW TO PAPER A ROOM

If a room has been papered several times, tear off all the loose parts you can and with a sponge and water loosen what remains on the walls, removing as much as possible, so as to have a smooth, even surface. If the room has never been papered, first go over it and fill all large cracks and holes with a paste made of whiting and water, or plaster of paris and water. When using the latter, mix only a little at a time, have it rather thin, and use quickly. Then, give the room a coat of sizing, which is made of common glue, three or four handfuls dissolved in a pail of boiling water. The sizing is applied with a large brush and should be allowed to dry overnight.

## Choose Judiciously

For very sunny rooms, select cool-looking papers, such as blues, greens and browns in various shades,

HANGING WALLPAPER

while for dark rooms pinks, reds, terra cottas and yellows are best. When selecting papers, pay careful attention to the color scheme of your room, and don't have an inharmonious mixture, which will offend good taste. Small, plain patterns are the most economical, and the easiest to match. The cheap, trashy papers, costing only a few cents a roll, are not worth the trouble of putting up. Gold paper is not to be recommended for wear.

No borders should be used for rooms having a low ceiling. For such, a striped paper of pretty design running right up to the ceiling is best. The ceiling may be papered in a plain or very small-patterned design, to harmonize with the side walls, or treated with several coats of tinted kalsomine or paint. A picture molding of appropriate color is used to finish the side walls, being placed scarcely 1 inch from the ceiling. The ceiling whether papered, painted or kalsomined, should be done first. It is a very difficult matter to paper the ceiling, and, unless you can have help, it would be better not to attempt it. Plain tints in paint or kalsomine are always pretty and in good taste. If, however, you want to risk papering the ceiling yourself, get some handy body to help you.

### Paste and Tools

The paste is made by simply boiling flour and water together, and adding a very little alum, salt and glue—about a tablespoon of each to a pound of flour. It should be of a consistency thick enough to apply easily, and not so thin that it will run.

Provide yourself with a good-sized paste brush, another one (a whitewash brush will do) to use dry over the paper, sharp scissors and a knife, plenty of clean rags, two barrels, two long, smooth, clean boards, each about 10 inches wide, and a stepladder.

Make a long table by placing the two barrels about 8 or 9 feet apart and on top of these the boards.

## Trimming and Cutting

The first thing to do is to cut the necessary number of strips of paper long enough to allow for waste in matching, and lay them all face downward on the "operating" table, one on top of the other. Next spread the paste evenly over the top or first strip of paper, being very sure to have the edges well pasted. Then turn top and bottom parts down, bringing pasted sides together, so that they meet, and none of the paste part is exposed, and carefully trim off edge on one side, with large, sharp scissors. Lift up the part thus trimmed and folded, and mount the ladder, which should previously have been placed convenient to the place where you intend to begin operations—the largest wall space is best, next to a door or window.

## Hanging the Paper

Now take hold of the top end which was doubled over (it will open and hang by its own weight) and adjust to its proper place on the wall. Then, with a large clean rag in your hand, rub downward, never up or sideways, and take great care to keep the edge straight. If you find that you didn't start straight from the top, loosen paper and do it over again. A "straight eye" is needed to do the work neatly. Don't rub too hard and always rub downward, doing a little part at a time, and lifting paper occasionally, so that no air bubbles are left under it. When the upper part is done, dismount from ladder, undo the folded part at the bottom of the width, and proceed in the same manner to adjust to the wall. When you are sure it is on straight and smooth, trim with a sharp knife along the base-board. Then give the strip another smoothing by going all over it again with a dry, clean brush. Proceed in this way until all the full length parts are covered, and then match in the small spaces over and below windows and doors. All the match-ing must be done with great care.

## Practical and Economical

Wainscoting in living or dining rooms are nice, and very practical, especially where there are small children. For this purpose burlap, or the less expensive dark, heavy papers that come in wood-grain imitation are good. Matting is sometimes used with very good effect, too. A narrow wooden molding is used to finish the top of the wainscoting, and in that case the work of papering the side walls is so much easier, the lengths being short.

## THE FARM BLACKSMITH SHOP

A blacksmith shop is of immense practical value on a farm. To those who have one it is almost as essential as live stock, farm tools and crops. One does not need to be a professional blacksmith. The elementary practice in welding, upsetting and tem-pering is easily learned with a little practice. Nor is it necessary to have many tools. An entire equip-ment may cost but a few dollars.

An old railroad rail will do for an anvil. But after getting the real article one is better satisfied and can do the work with greater ease. The forge should be obtained at the start. With it almost anyone can heat any small iron to welding point with as much ease as a regular blacksmith.

In the equipment of an Ohio farmer are a pair of tongs that he made himself, two other tongs and a large pair of pinchers picked up in a junk shop. He got the hammer and sledge from a hired man who had worked in a car shop. The anvil and vise also came from the junk shop, and both were in good repair. These cost $8, the hammer and sledge, $1.15, and an old, second-hand forge, $1.80. Not a large outlay to be sure, but a wise expenditure. If purchased at first hand the cost would be greater, but cheap at any price when you consider what you can do in the way of making and repairing with such a list of blacksmith tools.

In addition to the above list this man, Frank Ruhlen, has chisels, pinchers, fullers and other small tools, all of which he has made out of old pieces of steel taken from old worn-out machines. By figuring and planning just a little, any farmer can make the greater part of his own tools and at a very small cost for materials and labor.

## Why the Shop Pays

Mr. Ruhlen says: My shop was not started to replace the town blacksmith shop; and it will never do so. But it does serve for repair work, and it saves many trips to town. It is helpful in other ways, also. Last winter a sudden ice spell came on, so severe that I could not get the horses out to the field to feed the flock. Only one thing was possible: to have sharpened shoes put on the horses. But it was a disagreeable trip ahead to walk and lead the horses to town; so I decided to do the work myself. I had never set a shoe myself, but that trip before me quickly decided. The horses were brought into the shop, the old shoes pulled off and sharpened, and within an hour the feeding was done. Had I gone to town for the work it would have required time going and coming, and then, maybe a long wait ahead for my turn at the shop.

Last year I sharpened the shoes on the corn planter, and both cultivators, six shovels each. We wore out a steel point or shear, and never had it to shop but once, and then it was to get a new nose or point. I do not try to put steel points on anything, as it is too particular work for anyone who just picks tools up when something breaks. A sharp harrow is a luxury on most farms, because the average smith does not draw the teeth out enough, and they are dull in a few days.

And I do not believe the average smith can harden the farm tools as good as a farmer who has had some experience in tempering, as the farmer is the one who works with the tools, and soon learns when they are too hard or not hard enough. I sharpened my smoothing harrow last year before we commenced on our corn crop of 64 acres, used it on all the land, on some more than once, and my harrow is sharper now than my neighbor's, who paid $1.50 at the shop for the same work. We never use a dull mattock or pick now as we did before we had a forge. Welding chains, making chain hooks, open rings, clevises, are all easy to do on rainy days. I could not tell all the different uses I make of my shop.

## Blacksmithing Not Hired Man's Work

I do the work in the shop myself, finding other chores for hired men. You cannot afford to break them in, for the reason that they may soon leave and all the teaching and trouble would be for nothing. By doing the work myself, I have learned a little more each year, have acquired the knack of it, and really enjoy doing what is to be done. Had we had a shop when I was a boy all of the repair work could have been done by the boys, and I would at the same time have had splendid training for my own needs now.

My experience is all in favor of the shop on the farm. It pays well. Get the forge first, and then gradually add other tools as you can. I used a claw hammer for some time before getting a smith's hammer. I did not equip my shop all at once. Start in a small way, build up gradually, learn slowly, and the shop will develop itself. Get a shop, and you will believe in it because of its help to you.

## HORSESHOE LEVER

A handy lever for prying up boxes or barrels may be made by nailing an old horseshoe on the end of a 2 x 4, letting the ends of the horseshoe extend about an inch or two beyond the end of the timber. A more finished device may be constructed by cutting the upper part of the lever down to the form of a rounded handle. A horseshoe should be selected with fairly long and well-sharpened heel calks.

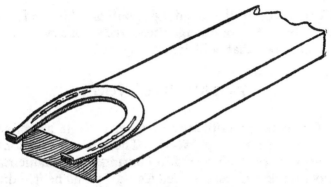

HORSESHOE FOR A TOOL

## HOW TO PAINT TIN ROOFS

Remove all rosin and other loose substances from seams and have roof clean. Paint immediately after laying is finished; do not allow the tin to rust—you coat the base plate with tin and lead to prevent rust, and paint the finished goods to prevent oxidation of the coating. Use only the best red or brown oxide of iron, mixed with pure linseed oil all raw, or half raw and half boiled. Use litharge only as a drier. Litharge makes paint adhere hard to coating, so that when thoroughly dry you cannot scrape it off. Don't use any turpentine or patent driers.

Apply all paint with hand brushes and rub in well. This is very important. Don't put paint on thick—one coat that covers well, and is thoroughly rubbed in, is better than three put on thick. Let roof stand two weeks to a month before applying second coat. Six months or so after applying second coat put on a third coat. After this you do not have to paint roof more than once every two or three years. Too much paint injures a tin roof.

Keep paint well stirred up; put on thin and rub well in. By following these directions you will have a roof that will last many years.

## PRESERVING WOOD

Creosote, or sulphate of copper or iron, are effective for preserving wood. There are objections, however, to their use for floorings or ornamental woodwork. Creosote leaves a permanent, disagreeable smell. The sulphates discolor the wood. Borax is excellent for keeping wood from decay. The preparation of it is simple, and consists in immersing the wood in a saturated solution of borax, which is then heated to 212 degrees Fahrenheit. The wood is left for 10 or 12 hours, the time depending upon the density and size of the pieces of wood. When taken out, the wood is stacked until dry, then reimmersed in a weaker solution of the borax for a brief time, dried again, and are then ready for use. Boards thus prepared are practically indestructible from rot, and are nearly incombustible.

Another preservative is a compound of one part silicate of potassa and three of pure water—the wood to remain in the solution 24 hours, then dried for several days, then soaked and dried a second time and afterward painted twice with a mixture of one part water-cement and four of the first-mentioned mixture. Thus prepared, it will not decay in the ground, and will be incombustible out of it.

Another process for preventing decay of wood is by use of a paint which possesses the advantages of being impervious to water. It is composed of 50 parts of tar, 500 parts of fine white sand, 4 parts of linseed oil, 1 part of the red oxide of copper in its native state, and 1 part of sulphuric acid. The tar, sand and oil should be first heated in an iron kettle; the oxide and acid are then added very carefully. The mass is thoroughly mixed and applied while hot. When dry, this paint is as hard as stone.

Decay in wood may be prevented by the following method: Take 20 parts of resin, 46 parts of finely powdered chalk, some hard sand, and a little linseed oil and sulphuric acid; mix and boil for a short time. If this is applied while hot, it forms a kind of varnish, thereby preserving the wood.

## TO PRESERVE SHINGLES

Following is an effective method to prevent the decay of shingles: Take a potash kettle or large tub and put into it one barrel of lye of wood ashes, 5 pounds of white vitriol, 5 pounds of alum, and as much salt as will dissolve in the mixture. Make the preparation quite warm, and put as many shingles in it as can be conveniently wet at once. Stir them up with a fork, and, when well soaked, take them out and put in more, renewing the preservative solution when necessary. Then lay the shingles in the usual manner.

After they are laid, take more of the preservative, put lime enough into it to make whitewash, and, if any coloring is desirable, add ocher, Spanish brown, lampblack, or other color, and apply to the roof with a brush or an old broom. This wash may be renewed from time to time.

Salt and lye are excellent preservatives of wood. Leach tubs, troughs and other articles used in the manufacture of potash never rot. They become saturated with the alkali, turn yellowish inside and remain impervious to the weather.

## TO RENDER WOOD FIREPROOF

Rendering the woodwork of houses secure against catching fire can be done at an insignificant cost, and with little trouble. Saturate the woodwork with a very delicate solution of silicate of potash as nearly neutral as possible, and when this has dried, apply one or two coats of a stronger solution.

Another method is simply to soak the wood with a concentrated solution of rock salt. Water-glass will act as well, but it is expensive. The salt also renders the wood proof against dry rot and the ravages of insects. Still another method is to immerse the wood in a saturated solution of borax, heat being gradually applied until the solution reaches 212 degrees Fahrenheit. It is then left for 10 or 12 hours, according to the nature and size of the wood.

## FIREPROOF WASH FOR SHINGLES

A preparation composed of lime, salt and fine sand or wood ashes, put on like whitewash, renders the roof 50 per cent more secure against taking fire from falling cinders, in case of fire in the vicinity. It pays the expense a hundredfold in its preserving influence against the effects of the weather. The older and more weather-beaten the shingles, the more benefit derived. Such shingles generally become more or less warped, rough and cracked; the application of the wash, by wetting the upper surface, restores them at once to their original form, thereby closing up the space between the shingles, and the lime and sand, by filling up the cracks and pores in the shingle itself, prevents warping.

## PETRIFIED WOOD

Mix equal parts of gem salt, rock alum, white vinegar, chalk and Peebles' powder. After the mixture becomes quiet, put into it any wood or porous substance, and the latter becomes like stone.

## HOW TO SEASON WOOD

Boiling small pieces of non-resinous wood will season them in four or five hours—the process taking the sap out of the wood, which shrinks nearly one-tenth in the operation. Trees felled in full leaf in June or July, and allowed to lie until every leaf has fallen, will then be nearly dry, as the leaves will not drop off themselves until they have drawn up and exhausted all the sap of the tree. The time required is from a month to six weeks, according to the dryness of the weather.

## BLEACHING WOOD

Sometimes it is more feasible to bleach a small part of a wood surface, especially in repairing, than to darken a larger portion of the work. This can be done by brushing over the wood a solution composed of 1 ounce oxalic acid in a pint of water, letting it remain a few minutes and then wiping dry. The operation may be repeated if necessary. A few drops of nitric ether, or a quarter of an ounce of tartaric acid, will assist the operation; or a hot solution of tartaric acid may be used alone. Lemon juice will also whiten most woods. Cut the lemon in half and rub the cut face upon the wood.

When the bleaching has been done and the wood is dry, give a thin coat of shellac or French polish, as the light and air acting upon the bare wood will bring back the original color.

If the wood obstinately resists bleaching, it may be lightened by mixing a little fine bismuth white, flake white or ball white (the cleansing balls sold by druggists) with the shellac, and give it a thin coat. This whitens, but it also somewhat deadens or obscures the grain and is, therefore, not so good as the bleaching method.

## WOOD POLISH

Rub evenly over the wood a piece of pumice stone and water until the rising of the grain is cut down; then take powdered tripoli and boiled linseed oil and polish to a bright surface.

## FURNITURE POLISH

Take equal parts of sweet oil and vinegar, mix, add a pint of gum arabic finely powdered. This will make furniture look almost as good as new and can be easily applied, as it requires no rubbing. The bottle should be shaken, and the polish poured on a rag and applied to the furniture.

## SIZE STAINS

By the aid of glue in the solution, the colors are fixed in size stains. They are employed for the purpose of giving a color to cheap work in soft woods, such as chairs, bedsteads and common tables and ordinary bookcases. The colors usually wanted are walnut, mahogany, cherry color, oak and even a rosewood.

For Mahogany—Dissolve 1 pound of glue in a gallon of water, and stir in ½ pound venetian red, and ¼ pound chrome yellow, or yellow ocher. Darken with the red and lighten with yellow, as desired. If the venetian red does not give a sufficiently dark look put in a pinch of lampblack. Apply hot.

For Rosewood—Same as mahogany, omitting the yellow, and using ¾ pound venetian red (or more) instead of ½ pound. Give one coat of this and then add lampblack, one pinch, or more, to the color; with the latter put in the figure or dark parts of the rosewood.

For Oak—In a gallon of glue size (as above) put ¾ pound powdered burnt umber. Lighten with yellow (chrome or ocher), if need be. Hot.

## DARK WOOD STAIN

White woods may be given the appearance of walnut by painting or sponging them with a concentrated warm solution of permanganate of potassa. Some kinds of wood become stained rapidly, while others require more time. The permanganate is decomposed by the woody fiber; brown peroxide of manganese is deposited, which afterward may be removed by washing with water. The wood, when dry, may be varnished, and will be found to resemble very closely the natural dark woods.

## RED STAIN FOR WOOD

Boil chopped Brazil wood thoroughly in water, strain it through a cloth. Then give the wood two or three coats, till it is the shade wanted. If a deep red is desired, boil the wood in water in which is dissolved alum and quicklime. When the last coat is dry, burnish it with the burnisher and then varnish.

## LIQUID GLUE

Dissolve 1 pound of best glue in 1½ pints of water, and add 1 pint of vinegar. It is ready for use.

## CEMENT FOR METAL AND GLASS

Take 2 ounces of a thick solution of glue, and mix it with 1 ounce of linseed-oil varnish, and half an ounce of pure turpentine; the whole is then boiled together in a close vessel. The two bodies should be clamped and held together for about two days after they are united to allow the cement to become dry. The clamps may then be removed.

## CEMENT FOR BROKEN CHINA

Stir plaster of paris into a thick solution of gum arabic till it becomes a viscous paste. Apply it with a brush to the fractured edges, and draw the parts closely together.

## CEMENT FOR CROCKERY AND GLASS

Take 4 pounds of white glue, 1½ pounds of dry white lead, ½ pound of isinglass, 1 gallon of soft water, 1 quart of alcohol, and ½ pint of white varnish. Dissolve the glue and isinglass in the water by gentle heat if preferred, stir in the lead, put the alcohol in the varnish and mix the whole together.

## MENDING GLASSWARE

Broken dishes and glassware may be easily mended as follows: Fit the pieces in their proper places and tie a string around the vessel to keep the parts from slipping out. Then boil the entire dish for two or three hours in sweet milk. This will firmly glue the vessel together and it will last for years with proper care.

## ARMENIAN CEMENT

This will strongly unite pieces of glass and china, and even polished steel, and may be applied to a variety of useful purposes. Dissolve five or six bits of gum mastic, each the size of a large pea, in as much rectified spirits of wine as will suffice to render it liquid; and, in another vessel, dissolve as much isinglass, previously a little softened in water (though none of the water must be used), in French brandy or good rum, as will make a two-ounce vial of very strong glue, adding two small bits of gum galbanum of ammoniacum, which must be rubbed or ground till they are dissolved. Then mix the whole with a sufficient heat. Keep the glue in a vial closely stopped, and when it is to be used set the vial in boiling water.

## JAPANESE CEMENT

Thoroughly mix the best powdered rice with a little cold water, then gradually add boiling water until a proper consistence is acquired, being particularly careful to keep it well stirred all the time; lastly it must be boiled for one minute in a clean saucepan or earthen pipkin. This glue is white, almost transparent, for which reason it is well adapted for fancy paper work, which requires a strong and colorless cement.

## ROOFING PREPARATION

Take 1 pint of fine sand, 2 of sifted wood-ashes, and 3 of lime ground up with oil. Mix thoroughly, and lay on with a painter's brush, first a thin coat, and then a thick one. This composition is not only cheap, but it strongly resists fire.

## FIRE KINDLERS

Take 1 quart of tar and 3 pounds of resin, melt them, bring to a cooling temperature, mix with as much sawdust, with a little charcoal added, as can be worked in; spread out while hot upon a board, when cold break up into lumps of the size of a large hickory nut, and you have, at a small expense, kindling material enough for one year. They will easily ignite from a match and burn with a strong blaze, long enough to start any wood that is fit to burn.

## MENDING PIPES WITH WATER ON

Many farmers have had trouble in repairing pipes where the water could not be shut off conveniently. A lead pipe which has been cut off accidentally in making an excavation, for instance, may be repaired by the following plan: The two ends of the pipe are plugged, and then a small pile of broken ice and salt are placed around them; in five minutes the water in the pipe will be frozen, the plugs removed, a short piece of pipe may then be inserted and perfectly soldered. In five minutes the ice in the pipes may be thawed and the water set to flowing freely again.

## TO JOIN WATER PIPES

Water pipes may be united by using a preparation made by combining four parts of good portland cement and one part of unslaked lime mixed together in small portions in a stout mortar, adding enough water to permit it to be reduced to a soft paste.

## WELDING METALS

Welding together two pieces of metal of any kind can be accomplished only when the surfaces to be joined are equally heated, and both surfaces must be brought to such a temperature that the particles will form a perfect continuity between the pieces united. This embraces the entire theory of welding, soldering or brazing metallic substances of any kind. In addition, however, to the equal and adequate heating of the surfaces to be united, every particle of coal dust, cinders or scales of oxide must be removed, so as to present two perfectly clean surfaces at the very moment when the union is to be effected.

The piece of metal that would fuse at the lower temperature must be the guide, when bringing the surfaces of conjunction up to the proper heat. If, for example, two pieces of wrought iron are to be welded, the part that will melt at the lower temperature must be brought just to a welding heat, and the surface of the other piece must be heated quite as hot, or a trifle hotter than the first piece. Then, if the surfaces are clean when the parts are brought together, the union will be satisfactory. The degree of heat aimed at must be, not to produce a fluid, but simply to bring the metal into a condition between the fluid and plastic.

## GRINDING TOOLS

All steel is composed of individual fibers running lengthways in the bar and held firmly together by cohesion. In almost all farm implements of the cutting kind the steel portion which forms the edge, if from a section of a bar, is welded to the bar lengthwise, so that it is the side of the bundle of fibers hammered and ground down that forms the edge. So, by holding on the grindstone all edge-tools, as axes, scythes and knives of strawcutters, in such a manner that the action of the stone is at right angles with the edge, or, this is to say, by holding the edge of the tools square across the stone, the direction of the fibers will be changed, so as to present the ends instead of the side as a cutting edge. By grinding in this manner a finer, smoother edge is set, the tool is ground in less time, holds an edge a great deal longer, and is far less liable to nick out and to break.

Plane irons should be ground to a level of about 35 degrees—chisels and gouges to 30. Turning chisels may sometimes run in an angle of 45. Molding tools, such as are used for ivory and for very hard wood, are made at from 50 to 60 degrees. Tools for working iron and steel are beveled at an inclination to the edge of from 60 to 70 degrees, and for cutting gun and similar metal range from 80 to 90.

# INDEX